Praise for Danny Abshire and *Natural Running*

"Danny Abshire is one of the lead voices in the natural running revolution."

—**Danny Dreyer, author of *ChiRunning***

"Running efficiently is a precursor to running any distance fast and exuberantly. No one knows this better than Danny Abshire, whose lifelong study of the body in motion has helped many champions reach their goals, me included. *Natural Running* is the definitive guide for anyone who craves the joy of effortless and timeless runs."

—**Lorraine Moller, four-time Olympian, Olympic bronze medalist, and cofounder of Lydiard Online Training Systems**

"Danny Abshire's approach gives hope to those who have struggled with injuries and uncomfortable running. He brings a simple, sensible, and usable approach to transforming your running so you can reach your potential. Danny's knowledge of running form and biomechanics can help all runners become more efficient."

—**Mark Allen, six-time Ironman® world champion and coauthor of *Fit Soul, Fit Body: 9 Keys to a Healthier, Happier You***

"Danny Abshire has devoted his professional life to studying and teaching proper and efficient running technique. He has worked with some of the best runners and triathletes in the history of endurance sports, and just speaking to him will make you a better runner."

—**Craig Alexander, two-time Ironman® world champion**

"For two decades Danny Abshire has been a lone voice in the wilderness, patiently showing the fortunate few the correct way to run. Now the rest of the running world gets the chance to learn from Abshire's running-form wisdom in *Natural Running*. With the pendulum finally swinging toward proper running shoes and technique, I e[...] standard reference source for years to com[...]

—**Mike Sandrock, author of *Running with the Le[...]***

"Danny Abshire has an innate knowledge of running biomechanics and an ability to translate his knowledge into a fix for running injuries."

—Paul Huddle, triathlon coach, contributor to *Triathlete* magazine, and author of *Start to Finish Ironman Training: 24 Weeks to an Endurance Triathlon*

"Danny Abshire is the leading authority on natural running form, period."

—Ian Adamson, seven-time Adventure Race world champion

"Danny Abshire is the true leader of the re-evolution back to more natural running."

—Mark Cucuzzella, MD, associate professor of family medicine, West Virginia University School of Medicine

"Danny Abshire's gifted instruction has excited my students at MIT for several years. His running clinics have inspired us to think about how we run and how to do so without pain. Danny can look at someone's running style; tweak it; and then make them a more efficient, faster running machine."

—Dr. Patti Christie, lecturer at Massachusetts Institute of Technology (MIT)

"Danny Abshire has a passion for helping people to run the way nature intended humans to run."

—Dr. Alexander Slocum, professor of mechanical engineering, MIT

natural
running

natural running

| the simple path to stronger, healthier running

| *by* danny abshire
| *with* brian metzler

Copyright © 2010 by Danny Abshire and Brian Metzler

All rights reserved. Printed in the United States of America.

No part of this book may be reproduced, stored in a retrieval system, or transmitted, in any form or by any means, electronic or photocopy or otherwise, without the prior written permission of the publisher except in the case of brief quotations within critical articles and reviews.

3002 Sterling Circle, Suite 100
Boulder, Colorado 80301-2338 USA
(303) 440-0601 · Fax (303) 444-6788 · E-mail velopress@competitorgroup.com

Distributed in the United States and Canada by Ingram Publisher Services

Library of Congress Cataloging-in-Publication Data
Abshire, Danny.
Natural running: the simple path to stronger, healthier running / Danny Abshire
with Brian Metzler.
    p. cm.
Includes bibliographical references and index.
ISBN 978-1-934030-65-3 (pbk.: alk. paper)
1. Running—Training. I. Metzler, Brian. II. Title.
GV1061.5.A27 2010
796.42—dc22

                                                          2010043296

For information on purchasing VeloPress books, please call (800) 811-4210 ext. 2138 or visit www.velopress.com.

This paper meets the requirements of ANSI/NISO Z39.48-1992 (Permanence of Paper).

Cover design by Don Gura
Cover illustration by Marty Smith
Interior design and composition by Jessica Xavier
Illustrations by Susan Decker; illustrations on pp. 62 and 83 based on a concept by Terra Plana
All photos by Brian Metzler except p. 85 by Mark Doolittle, p. 97 by Getty Images, p. 11 by iStockphoto, and pp. 17 and 75 by Brad Kaminski

13   14   15 / 10   9   8   7   6

I dedicate this book to my wife, Jennifer Abshire. Without Jennifer's strong belief in me and my work, this book would not be possible.

Contents

Foreword

I met Danny Abshire in 1993, when at the height of my triathlon career I suffered a potentially career-ending injury: an extremely serious stress fracture in my ankle. I had been told through all conventional channels that there was no way back to world-class running and competing. A good friend told me about Danny and his company, Active Imprints, in Boulder, Colorado, and how he had helped her. As a desperate professional athlete who had exhausted every other avenue, from physical therapy to magnets, lasers, and herbal concoctions, I headed straight to Boulder to see this "guru."

Using an amazingly logical approach, Danny quickly and easily "saw" what no one else had been able to see. By identifying and adjusting light-weight custom orthotics for an unbalanced forefoot alignment, Danny made simple biomechanical and structural adjustments that resolved six months of pain and ended my agonizing over the future of my career as an athlete. Having been told just weeks earlier that I would never run competitively again, I went on to win a sixth Ironman® world championship just two months later—a result that no amount of praise can do justice. Fast forward to another three world championships and years of injury-free running and racing.

I invited Danny to be a guest speaker and running form coach/biomechanics instructor at the Multisports.com training camps held around the United States. We wanted to help the age-group runner and triathlete stop overstriding and learn to land under the body safely, ultimately to become a more efficient runner. Danny did this and more and also inspired thousands of runners to stay in the moment and not think so far ahead, listen to their bodies, and use their minds accordingly.

My relationship and partnership with Danny continues today. It's a privilege to know someone who is clearly gifted with an understanding of all things biomechanical. I have watched him be the spark in so many lives, enabling athletes at every level in any sport to pursue their goals. Danny has been and continues to be a source of inspiration for me.

Danny and this book will inspire you, as he has countless others, to open your mind and rethink the way you currently run and will set you on a course to becoming a more efficient and natural runner, as you were meant to be.

The story of Paula Newby-Fraser and my career both as an athlete and a coach cannot be told without Danny Abshire's starring role.

—Paula Newby-Fraser

Acknowledgments

No one, other than my wife, has had as much belief in me as Jerry Lee. Jerry and his wife, Donna, are incredibly giving people who helped me believe that we could create a company that built running shoes specifically for natural running form. We hoped to reduce injury rates and create a more enjoyable running experience for runners all over the world. With a focus on giving back to the community—and to the world as it grows—Newton is a charitable company thanks to the Jerry and Donna Lee Family Foundation.

The athletes and coaches at the Multisports.com training camps also believed in me; starting in 1993, they encouraged me to coach running biomechanics, injury prevention, and running form. My deepest thanks go especially to Paula Newby-Fraser, Paul Huddle, Heather Fuhr, Roch Frey, and Jimmy Riccitello for using Active Imprints custom orthotics to boost their own athletic performance and for allowing me to coach thousands of runners through their triathlon camps. They also were part of our original testing group for Newton running shoes.

A big thank-you goes to Brian Metzler for his invaluable assistance in crafting the language of this book and for guiding me down the technical trail of writing.

Finally, to all the running coaches around the world with open minds who have worked hard for many years with little credit to help runners adjust their form to a more natural running style—thank you, and keep up the good work!

Introduction

Evolution to a Running Revolution

I have been a runner all my life, dating back to my youth in Tennessee, when I enjoyed dashing through the forest, dodging trees, and feeling the uninhibited excitement and freedom of movement while coexisting with nature. I have vivid memories of running in junior high school, relishing the self-generated speed from wearing a pair of spikes on a cinder track. I remember what it was like later, in high school, to jet across a man-made surface—the dramatic forward lean, high cadence, and excitement of moving as fast as possible over short distances.

In time I started training for distance running as opposed to sprinting and found a peaceful challenge to running more miles. When I ran my very first distance race, a 5-miler, I found myself both exhilarated and utterly spent from the all-out effort. For the first time I really saw and felt how your mind can push your body beyond what you think you're capable of physically. I quickly forgot the soreness and fatigue of the event and relished the euphoria and relative peace of the run and the overall challenge of the event. It was the coolest thing I'd ever done, and I was hooked. I thought about running all the time and wanted to run faster and farther—so, a little like Forrest Gump, that was what I did.

I graduated from high school in 1975 and like a lot of teens wasn't sure what I wanted to do with my life. A friend told me about this place in Colorado that she had driven through on a recent road trip, and it sounded like a great place to get a job and take a break before I had to contemplate what to do with my life. So I sold my beat-up Austin-Healy Sprite for 300 bucks and left for Aspen, Colorado.

Like most mountain-town refugees, I took up skiing and really enjoyed the speed and freedom. I have to give credit to my roommate Chip Simons for teaching me. He was a truly awesome skier, someone who made it look easy—skiing fast with perfect form and always in total control.

One of my first days, he took me to the top of the mountain and said I'd better listen up lest I break something or kill myself. "Do you know where your center is?" he asked. I had no idea what that meant. "Your center of mass, the center of your body," he said. He told me to close my eyes and imagine the vertical midpoint of my body. I followed his instructions and told him I figured it was at my belly button or perhaps slightly lower.

He concurred and then had me stand up straight, lock my knees, and put my skis close together. He then asked if I was centered. I said sure, but then he put one finger on my shoulder and pushed me down hard into the snow. "What the hell, Chip? If this is how someone learns to ski, it sucks!" He laughed and helped me up. Then he told me to stand with my feet at about shoulder width, flex my ankles and knees, hold my arms at my sides with my elbows at 90 degrees, and look forward. He grabbed me by the shoulder and tried to push me down, but because of my centered, balanced, athletic position, I was able to react and stay balanced, offsetting his attempts to topple me. He laughed again and said I learned pretty quick for a Tennessee boy.

I fell several times, but by the end of that day I was tackling challenging black-diamond runs at the Aspen Highlands. I'd been thrown into the deep end and learned how to survive thanks to Chip's instruction and key points about proper form and technique.

I got work in a local ski shop, first in the rental department, then in sales and ski tuning, before I eventually became a professional ski-boot fitter. The job was about helping the customer find comfort while still having a firm control on performance, but it was a gig that would never interest most people because of the pain, anger, frustration, and hopelessness thousands of skiers experience with their boots every year. To me, each customer was like a puzzle to be figured out, although not easily in most cases.

Early in the job, I started looking at every foot as unique, noting the differences between right and left and stabilizing them accordingly with foot supports in both the heel and forefoot. I adjusted canting (the vertical angle of the lower leg) to make sure the center of the knee mass was over the center of the foot and ski. I'd heat, shape, grind, and stretch the boot material to match the newly balanced foot.

I picked up pointers from other boot fitters, but I also developed my own tricks and techniques based on what I was learning about the biomechanics of skiing. My approach started from a simple concept: To ski properly, you must have a level foot position to stand flat on a ski. By this I mean the heel and ball of the foot must be balanced. Think of how stable a camera tripod is when properly balanced. Without this level foot position, it's very difficult to track level on your skis, make a right or left turn, or stop quickly by applying pressure to the ski edges.

So began my interest in understanding not only what the foot is capable of but also how a balanced forefoot and an athletic position were necessary for virtually every sport as well as being the most effective position for everyday activities from walking upstairs to raking leaves. I was able to work with some of the top ski-boot fitters and custom ski-boot insole makers in the world. And so, for 10 years, I happily spent winters skiing, making custom insoles, and adjusting ski boots and summers doing odd jobs and focusing on running. With the running boom in full swing and more and more races popping up, I became increasingly interested in running longer-distance races and embarked on training for my first marathon.

Footwear was changing, too. Running shoes were becoming softer, and the heel height was becoming higher to accommodate new midsole cushioning technologies such as air and gel bags, which were meant to cushion runners from the hard surfaces of road running. One of the by-products of the heel height increase was that runners started to lead or strike with their heels first. That made the foot a loose adapter, which allows the ankle to roll in or out to adapt to changes in the surface, and meant that the foot was unable to relay to the brain from its interaction with the ground how the rest of the body should be positioned. Not surprisingly, excessive pronation and supination (terms I explain in detail in Chapter 2) of the ankle started to affect runners negatively.

In fact, the change in my own running style led to one of my first running injuries, plantar fasciitis, prompting me to question whether runners really needed more support in their running shoes. I surmised that they didn't need a rigid orthotic provided by the medical industry that focused on the rear foot, but rather something like the ski insoles that I had made for years to keep skiers balanced and in control of their skis. I realized way back then that being balanced and centered with gravity is the best starting point for any sport, including and especially running.

An understanding of the biomechanics of running was all coming together for me back in 1984, which was also the year I ran my first marathon, the Colorado Marathon in Grand Junction. Unlike the huge marathon crowds of today, there were just about 150 of us who ran out of town into the quiet, lonely desert amid the desolate rock mesas of western Colorado. I was determined to run the race in 3 hours or less, but a severe cant on the two-lane rural desert highway began to take its toll. I started to get uncomfortable mentally and physically and tried to find flat ground to spell myself from the continuous slope. Pulling into 20 miles, I was on a 2-hour, 55-minute pace, but the wheels were about to fall off.

I felt my iliotibial (IT) band begin to tighten as a result of too much forefoot medial rotation from the slope of the road. I not only hit the wall at 22 miles, I got crushed by the course. Hobbled by my right leg, I shifted my weight to my left leg and adjusted my goal from less than 3 hours to simply finishing. The weight shift to my left side made my left lateral ankle start to give in to the cant as well. "Overcompensation" was a term I would later come to understand.

I finished in 3:12 and had to walk with a ski pole as a crutch for over a week with ice packs taped to my ankle and knee. I'd found out the painful way how angles under your feet, either natural or unnatural, can cause alignment problems for the body. I learned that overcompensating for one problem will lead to the next, and when I got back home I made myself my first arch supports for running.

That same year, I met my wife-to-be, Jennifer, who was visiting from Canada. We married two years later and moved from Aspen to Boulder in 1988 to start Active Imprints, a service business that made foot supports. We would make them for every sport as well as for daily comfort in casual and work shoes. We presented our services to the University of Colorado's athletic department, and soon we were working with its football, ski, and track teams.

Our mission was to develop lightweight custom foot supports, built for any sport in about an hour. No matter the sport, at high performance levels feet must be balanced to provide proper alignment, maximize power output, and reduce rotational forces (which create wear and tear on the body). It didn't take long for Jennifer and me to get acquainted with many of the top national- and world-class athletes who gather in Boulder.

I also became involved with many podiatrists, orthopedists, physical therapists, chiropractors, and massage therapists who saw the benefits of a lightweight, more flexible foot support incorporating forefoot correction and started referring injured athletes and clients to us. Jennifer and I were asked to speak at Denver hospitals and clinics on injury prevention, foot support, and how to match particular running shoes with particular problems. We also worked with training camps focusing on running form and foot biomechanics.

We were working with many injured recreational runners as well as world-class athletes from almost every sport, who began asking our opinion about particular injuries. I first met New Zealander Lorraine Moller in 1991. Lorraine had a very high arch, and years of long-distance running and racing had put strain on her Achilles tendon. When she came to me in 1991 a heel spur, or sharp, bony prominence, had formed on the heel bone, causing her to overcompensate and roll inward to avoid pain.

X-rays revealed a whopping half-inch heel spur sticking into her Achilles tendon. As an Olympic marathoner, she had only two options: stop running or have the spur removed. And stopping wasn't really an option! She had the spur removed and began the challenge of rehabilitation with an eye toward the Barcelona Olympics the following year.

Progress was slow, from healing internally and externally to walking, pool running, and finally back to basic training. I made a series of foot supports for her that started with some heel height to take stress off the tendon and gradually brought the heel down. A patient and persistent athlete, Lorraine did what she needed to do and no more. Her patience, hard work, and dedication to recovery and retraining paid off: She won the bronze medal despite adverse heat and humidity in Barcelona. An amazing runner, she has raced in four Olympic marathons, winning a bronze medal for her country at age 37 in Barcelona in 1992 and competing respectably again at age 41 in Atlanta.

Lorraine and athletes like her inspire me, and indeed the work of my life has been fueled by my passion for helping athletes improve their mechanics for optimal fitness and performance; reducing the chance for injuries; and, perhaps most important, maximizing the joy of running. After all, those are the reasons we all run, right? Those same motivating factors also led me to design custom lightweight orthotics and running shoes geared toward helping people run better, more efficiently, and faster with fewer injuries.

In the process of helping athletes perform better and reduce injuries, we discovered that, although there is no such thing as perfect form, there *is* a better way to run, a more optimal kind of running mechanics. By the 1990s I was developing my lectures around three things: running form, foot type, and minimum range of motion. As I will explain in great detail in this book, those three factors are the keys to understanding and avoiding most of the common injuries caused by excessive braking, rotational, and propulsive forces.

After many years of research and design, I cofounded Newton Running in 2007 with the explicit goal of creating the first running shoe based on physics and the biomechanics of natural human running motion. I also wanted Newton Running to be the first company to talk about and teach natural running form as a way to help runners relearn how to run—or, in some cases, to learn to run for the first time. After three years in business, we've put runners on the path to new personal records (PRs) and healthier running and helped Craig Alexander win a pair of Ironman triathlon world championships. Although I'm pleased to have played a part in the victories he and other Newton athletes have racked up, I'm just as proud of the thousands of testimonials from runners who have e-mailed to tell me how much the shoes and improved natural running form have enhanced their running.

Although partially prompted by recent research and mainstream appeal, this book represents a 30-year accumulation of scientific information, logic, and firsthand experience derived from studying the feet, biomechanics, and injury patterns of thousands of runners as well as building custom insoles for runners of all abilities and developing innovative shoes for Newton Running.

Natural Running is about teaching people how to run better, more efficiently, and with fewer injuries. It comes at a time when there are more people running than ever before; more people using running as their primary form of fitness; and more people training for 5Ks, 10Ks, half-marathons, marathons, and ultradistance events. Yet although running shoes have evolved tremendously since the 1970s, injury rates among runners have not subsided.

My goal in these pages is not to effect industrywide change but instead to offer a path to individual running enlightenment and improvement. This book doesn't offer a miracle cure, training shortcuts, or immunity from injuries. But through a close examination of running shoes, the biomechanics of the feet, the science of motion, and the physics of running, it provides vital cues for healthier running that can ultimately lead to more enjoyment, greater longevity as an athlete, and possibly faster race times. My deepest hope is that the passion, experience, and insight I have tried to bring to this book will help you discover—or perhaps rediscover—the pure joy and euphoria of natural running.

1

What Is Natural Running?

Running is one of the most natural things we do as human beings. We were, quite literally, born to run. From prehistoric days, when running ensured survival, to today, when more people are pounding the pavement for fitness and pleasure than ever before, running has long been a part of the very fabric of who we are. Very little compares to the euphoria of being fit and feeling good out on a run. With a breeze in your face and everything else in your dust, running is at once invigorating and calming, inspiring and transcending.

But if running is so natural, why do so many runners end up sidelined? Why is the running population getting slower? Training programs, shoes, and running gear are highly advanced, seemingly giving runners every advantage, especially compared to when the running boom began in the 1970s. So why have median marathon finishing times gotten longer? And why are more runners getting injured than ever before? The American Medical Athletic Association reports that every year 37 to 50 percent of runners suffer running injuries severe enough to reduce or stop training or cause them to seek medical care (Wilk et al. 2009; Van Mechelen 1994).

With almost 44 million runners in the United States (according to a 2009 survey by the Sports Goods Manufacturers Association), that percentage range means 16 to 22 million runners are getting hurt every year. Compare that to a 1989 study that reported 48 percent of runners suffered some sort of running injury annually (Van Middelkoop et al. 2008). Twenty years of more advanced shoes and training plans, but the same number of injuries? What gives?

There has to be a better way, a healthier way, to enjoy such a primal, euphoric, and truly natural activity, whether your goal is reaching a new personal best in a marathon or simply enjoying an easy jog a few times a week to stay fit.

There *is* a better way to run. It's called natural running, which is in essence running the way your body was meant to run: purely, efficiently, and uninhibitedly.

Natural running is not a new concept. In fact, it has been around since at least as far back as that first Neanderthal 10K. As barefoot runners chasing down sustenance in prehistoric times, humans more than likely ran with an upright form, a compact arm swing, a high cadence, and foot strikes at their midfoot below their center of mass, rather than crashing to the ground with their heels on every step. We know this because that's how the human body moves most efficiently and economically when unshod or (perhaps) in thin-soled animal-skin slippers on natural surfaces. Two million years of evolution haven't changed how we were intended to run. Anatomy just hasn't evolved that much, according to Dr. Daniel Lieberman, an evolutionary biologist and professor who runs the Skeletal Biology Lab at Harvard University and has closely studied the impacts of barefoot running. Lieberman's landmark 2010 study (Lieberman et al. 2010) in essence proved that we haven't lost the ability to run naturally. His study is one of many recent research endeavors showing that human beings run more efficiently and with less impact while running barefoot than in shoes.

The problem is not that we have forgotten how to run naturally; it's more that we have fallen prey to unnatural influences in the modern world—namely running shoe designs and the hard surfaces we typically run on. The good news is that by understanding what natural running

Figure **1.1** | *This boy runs on the beach in the most pure and natural way.*

form is and how to readapt to it, you can rediscover the way you were meant to run.

Imagine yourself running barefoot across the soft grass of a soccer field or along the smooth, wet sand at the beach (see Figure 1.1). This evokes a good feeling, right? No matter how fast or experienced you are as a runner or what your level of fitness is today, you'll more than likely be transported back to a simpler time in your life. You will simply run, naturally, smoothly, efficiently. Nothing more, nothing less. Your body will move freely and easily, your limbs in harmony with your feet, almost as if you're skimming across the surface of the earth. Why is this? Because that's the way your body has been designed to move. It's only through the advent of modern footwear—especially overcushioned running shoes— that we have (recently) evolved as heavy heel-strikers.

No matter how fast you're running, your body is in harmony with the ground beneath you, moving freely and easily, springing almost effort-lessly with each footstep as you move from point A to point B. Muscles in your legs and core engage easily to continue your forward momentum, and like your ancient ancestors, you are probably running with an upright posture and a slight forward lean; a compact, consistent arm swing; and low-impact footsteps near the ball of your foot.

Your body uses the sensory feedback gained from each foot's interaction with the ground to help you move as safely and efficiently as possible over any surface. That interaction, known as *afferent feedback*, is gained from an area under the forefoot section of your foot, where your body is naturally and most effectively balanced with gravity for any type of athletic movement.

The moment your forefoot senses the ground, your brain uses that feedback and positions your body to run as efficiently and in as balanced a way as possible. Within that foot–brain interaction, there is an understanding that the soft surface is not only safe but will help cushion the impact of each footstep and accommodate the position of your foot. That's natural running in a natural world.

Now picture yourself running barefoot across a sidewalk, street, or wood floor. Because your brain interprets the potential danger of the hard surface beneath your feet (which will offer no cushioning to help reduce the impact of each step), it naturally puts you in position to run with very light foot strikes that will help you avoid the blunt force trauma of hitting the concrete or another hard surface. To do that, you'll land at the midfoot/forefoot portion of your foot (the ball of the foot, but not the toes) and quickly lift your foot off the ground instead of pushing off with excessive muscular force. I call this self-regulating your impact. Your brain knows from both instinct and experience that landing on your heels while running barefoot on a hard surface will result in painful and debilitating injury. Your body isn't engineered to accommodate the trauma of repeated heel striking, which is why you naturally avoid a heel-striking gait, especially on harder surfaces. That's natural running adapting to an unnatural world.

In sum, natural running is running the way the human body was meant to run in its purest form across any surface, smooth, soft, jagged, or hard. Because we run in overbuilt footwear in an unnatural world full of concrete, pavement, and even hard-packed dirt trails that aren't necessarily safe for bare feet, we need to relearn how to run naturally, wearing lightweight shoes that offer some degree of protection while allowing us to mimic the sensation of running barefoot.

Running 101

Almost anyone can run, no matter how fit or athletically inclined. Many people take up running because it seems so uncomplicated compared to other sports. You really don't need a lot of expensive equipment, you don't have to go anywhere but out your front door to participate, you don't have to pay dues to an exclusive club, and you don't have to take lessons to get started. Most people figure that if they invest in a pair of running shoes and put in some sweat equity by running every day, the returns of improved health, increased happiness, and a self-generating, lifelong passion are almost guaranteed.

Although running is certainly one of the most accessible sports you can pursue, this kind of oversimplification has sidelined countless runners. Millions of people have signed up for races and run marathons, but few have actually considered the importance of good form or training. You take lessons on how to better swing a golf club or a tennis racket, or to learn the proper techniques for shooting a basketball or throwing a curve ball, but what about running? You might have finished a marathon— or several—but unless you're an elite athlete, chances are you've never been instructed how to run properly. You might follow a detailed online program, do workouts with a local running group, or even follow a training plan from an expert coach. But preparation for a race, whether it's a 5K or a marathon, is typically focused on different types of workouts, not on how you should actually run.

Does it really matter how you run? Yes, because if you run without learning proper form, you could wind up being woefully inefficient, and worse yet, set yourself up for a variety of debilitating injuries. Two of the biggest mistakes distance runners fall prey to are (1) running with a heel strike, which causes abrupt braking of forward momentum and leads to excessive rotation in feet, ankles, knees, legs, and hips; and (2) using too much muscular force to create forward propulsion. Each of these form flaws contributes to too much vertical oscillation in every stride, which leads to inefficiency and considerably more impact, rotation, and muscle and tendon stress on the body.

Common Running Form Mistakes

Braking Impact/Excessive Rotation. If you find yourself landing hard on your heels and braking your forward momentum on every stride, you are overstriding. This means your foot isn't landing below your center of mass, so your ankle is relegated to being a loose adapter, which allows for excessive rotational forces. As your foot is free to roll inward or outward, so too are your ankle, lower leg, knee, upper leg, hips, and spine. By running that way, you're putting various muscles, joints, and soft tissues at risk of overuse injuries from the excessive rotation that starts in your foot and goes up your body. Also, this type of landing increases impact forces to the heel, knee, hip, and lower back.

Excessive Muscular Force. If you're running with a heel-striking gait and braking your forward momentum on every stride, you need extra muscular force to regenerate that momentum. With every heel-strike *in front of* your center of mass, your upper body is pushed backward *behind* your center of mass.

That compromised position causes you to spend extended time on the ground from the heel-strike phase to the mid-stance phase (discussed in Chapter 4) of your gait as your upper body moves forward and becomes balanced over your midfoot. Now you need to push off hard with excessive muscular force to maintain your relative speed. As you push off your toes like a sprinter, your propulsive muscles (the calf muscle group, hamstrings) and the connective tissue of your lower leg, ankle, and foot (primarily the plantar fascia and Achilles tendon) will be in jeopardy of fatiguing, straining, or injury.

These two form mistakes are common responses to being out of balance with gravity, which is often the case when running in overbuilt running shoes with a high heel lift on unnatural surfaces. It's not that you can't run this way; you might be comfortable running in an inefficient manner and maybe you have even set a new marathon PR running this way. After all, for the past 30 years most running shoes have had a high heel lift that has encouraged heel striking. But if you are running somewhat efficiently with a very inefficient form, your running economy (the ability to process oxygen efficiently while running) is negatively affected because you're expending considerably more energy mitigating the hard impacts and pushing off to begin a new stride.

Combined, these two form mistakes contribute to the most common running overuse injuries, including shin splits, plantar fasciitis, Achilles tendonitis, iliotibial band issues, and patellofemoral pain. Those injuries can be frustrating by-products of what should be an otherwise enjoyable and healthy experience. You might get away with running inefficiently for years, but it *will* eventually catch up with you.

If this is the way you've been running, or if you have suffered overuse injuries, don't despair. You can learn a better way to run. Natural running is based on how your feet move when you run barefoot. Though that doesn't mean you should ditch your shoes and start running barefoot today, you can certainly improve your form, become a stronger runner, and run more efficiently, as if you were running barefoot.

Rediscovering Your Natural Running Form

Running barefoot is the most primal form of natural running. It takes us back to our primitive roots, but also back to our own youthful moments of running across a carpeted floor as a toddler; through a soft, grassy park as a juvenile; or along the shoreline of a sandy beach as an adolescent. And although we have moved on, both as a human species and from childhood to adolescence and eventually to adulthood, that primal connection to natural running remains. Natural running is engrained in all of us and always will be, even though our current fitness levels, relatively sedentary lifestyles, inappropriate shoes, abnormal injuries, and other variables of the unnatural, modern world make it seem hopelessly remote. Despite bad habits, bodily changes, and dangerous surfaces, natural running is absolutely attainable if we take the appropriate steps to find and nurture it.

Though its roots are ancient, only in recent years has barefoot running attained mainstream notoriety and science-based credibility. Christopher McDougall's best-selling *Born to Run* (2009), combined with the completion of numerous scientific studies, set forth in the mainstream media the idea that most runners need to reexamine how they run and exposed the negative influence that modern footwear has had on the act of running.

For years, high-level runners from around the world have used barefoot running in small doses to develop proprioception (the body's ability to sense the ground and immediately react by positioning and moving itself accordingly), improve balance, and strengthen the small muscles in their feet and lower legs, especially as preparation for running in ultralight racing shoes or track spikes. Those muscles are typically underutilized and even deconditioned while running in shoes with thick midsoles and a high heel lift and therefore can't do what they are supposed to do—absorb impact force, control rotational forces, and release stored energy—a problem that is compounded by the fact that most of us wear soft or heel-lifted shoes nearly all the time, both at work and play.

The Shoe's Impact on Form

If you wear a high-heel running shoe, which most recreational runners do today, it is very difficult to run with natural running form. But running shoes weren't always built that way. At the start of the American running boom in the early 1970s, most people were running in lightweight shoes that consisted of a rubber outsole, a thin foam midsole, and a lightweight nylon upper. Although simple by today's standards, some of those early shoes were pretty good at letting the foot and body move naturally without the need for excessive muscular force. Those shoes also allowed a runner to obtain valuable sensory feedback from the foot's interaction with the ground and to self-regulate impact.

As footwear technology advanced over the years, running shoes generally became cushier, softer, thicker, and heavier. Heel heights increased to accommodate new midsole cushioning technologies such as air bags and gel packets meant to cushion runners from the hard surfaces of road running. Compared to the original running shoes of the mid-1960s or to the animal-skin moccasins of primitive peoples, running shoes started to look almost cartoonish.

Figure **1.2** │ *Cutaway of standard running shoe showing a 14.7 percent rise in ramp angle from toe to heel*

Although some of the design innovations were driven by performance, the end result in many cases was anything but performance oriented. And that's why, more than 30 years later, thousands of people run with inefficient mechanics predicated on a heel-striking gait. Not only is that form not optimal for running fast, it can lead to numerous overuse injuries. But beyond that, the excessive pounding and pushing caused by constantly braking and using muscular force to start a new stride leaves the runner with a debilitating feeling that is contrary to the exhilarating sensation of running with natural, efficient form.

Large, overbuilt heel crash pads and steep heel-to-toe ramp angles (see Figure 1.2) in modern shoe design are the biggest culprits in allowing, and in fact encouraging, a heel-striking gait—especially for those new to the sport who haven't had instruction or experience with more efficient mechanics. Even if you want to run with a natural midfoot/forefoot stride pattern, the geometry and heel height of many shoes will not allow your foot to land naturally—namely parallel to the ground—because the hefty heel gets in the way. It's the first thing that hits the ground as your foot swings through the gait cycle. Another problematic aspect is the soft foam midsole, which dampens the foot's sensory intake (because it's harder to feel the ground), thus thwarting the relay of information back to the brain about how the rest of the body should be positioned. So if shoes are the problem, shouldn't we all just run barefoot? Yes and no.

Barefoot Running

If you're used to running in a shoe with a built-up heel, running barefoot can be a fascinating experience of freedom and the first step in developing natural running mechanics. Running unshod, your foot naturally seeks out the ground by landing at the midfoot, where it receives afferent feedback and immediately tells the body how to move as efficiently and effectively as possible. That same feedback can be gained while wearing shoes, but it is considerably dampened by thick levels of foam and much harder to interpret with a heel-striking gait.

So what about running barefoot all the time? No way, say most doctors, podiatrists, physical therapists, coaches, and elite runners, who concur that it's neither practical nor safe to run barefoot. Running barefoot for several miles on a paved road or concrete sidewalks sounds terribly painful, not to mention impractical and even dangerous. I'm not saying you can't, but you could be setting yourself up for other injuries if you do.

However, under controlled circumstances, barefoot running can be quite good for you, whether you're an elite athlete, a new runner, or somewhere in between. Done regularly in small doses, barefoot running can improve your mechanics and teach your body to land lightly at your midfoot, even while wearing shoes. I discuss barefoot running as an effective training tool more thoroughly in Chapter 9.

The principle behind barefoot running makes a lot of sense, but so does the principle behind shoes. Most of us don't live in a part of the world where soft dirt roads or sandy beaches connect towns and cities. Our modern world is heavily paved and therefore not conducive to running barefoot. Shoes will protect your feet from hazards like glass, gravel, and debris, and wearing shoes gives you thermal properties that are lacking when you run barefoot on hot pavement or frozen sidewalks. The bottom line is that although running barefoot in small doses can help make you a better natural runner, it isn't the answer. A better solution is to run with lightweight shoes that allow your feet to mimic the flexibility and motion of barefoot running while still offering protection from unnatural surfaces and helping to transfer downward energy into forward propulsion.

Adopting Natural Running

Natural running will make you a stronger, more efficient runner. This book is about teaching you how to do that. It doesn't offer miracle cures, training shortcuts, or immunity from injury. Instead, it will help you help yourself, by better understanding the physics of running and the science of the foot, while showing you how to transition to natural running gradually and teaching you how to maintain that form for the rest of your life. Natural running is all about feet, form, and whole body freedom. The key is running in a relaxed manner and having the awareness to touch the ground lightly with each footstep, lifting quickly on every stride. Combined with an upright posture that includes a slight lean at the waist and a compact arm swing, this stride leads to the optimally efficient running mechanics your body is predisposed to, which can result in less impact and fewer rotational forces on the foot and body.

There's no such thing as perfect running form, but we can all work on running mechanics and improving efficiency. Doing so will make you a more efficient runner, which means you'll use less energy in every stride and boost your running economy. Ultimately, improved form can make you faster.

Adopting natural running isn't difficult, but it takes focus and a commitment to replacing old, familiar habits, which can be challenging to break, with new ones. Understanding and improving your running mechanics, getting lightweight training shoes that are better suited for a natural running gait, and working continually on building and maintaining your strength and technique with drills are all part of the process of becoming an informed runner and thereby a better one.

The first part of this book explores some of the relevant history of running and the significant impacts of the evolution of running shoes on running form. Then I take you into my lab, where we take a closer look at how the human body moves, the biomechanics of the foot, and the physics of natural running as well as examine common running injuries, how they occur, and how they can be avoided. Finally, I make all of this applicable to you and your running, helping you transition to a more natural style of running with practical tips, specific drills, and an eight-week training plan.

One of the primary ways to improve your running technique is through form drills. Form drills are easy to do and don't take a lot of time, but they're often overlooked, forgotten, or ignored when a workout is completed. Taking an extra 5 to 15 minutes to do form drills several times per week will make you more fluid, more efficient, and even faster for both short and long distances.

Most drills take the aspects of good form—a compact arm swing, soft foot strikes with the foot under your center of mass, quick leg turnover, an upright posture with a slight forward lean at the waist—and accentuate these in a quick, repetitive motion that trains the body to be comfortable with those movements during your regular running mechanics. Some drills are aimed at building smaller muscles (such as the intrinsic group and lumbrical group in the foot), while others help your neuromuscular system fire quicker.

Transitioning to natural running isn't the same for any two people. For some, it might entail fixing a few bad habits, making better choices with footwear, and committing to the form drills. For others, it might require starting from scratch and forgetting everything you thought you knew about running. But fear not, the transition to natural running can begin immediately—as soon as today—and it's not overly complex. It might take time and adherence to detail, but the end result will make you a stronger, healthier, and quite possibly faster runner. More than that, it will help you tap into a newfound enthusiasm and euphoria perhaps missing up to now in your running. So have patience. Once you learn to run naturally, you'll run faster and healthier not just for today, but for the rest of your life.

2
Evolution of a Sport and a Shoe

Human beings have been running since prehistoric times, first for the necessity of survival, then as a way to prove their dominance among tribespeople, and eventually for sport. Running races were part of many ancient civilizations and have been a staple of modern societies since the Renaissance. Today's marathon boom has its roots in the rebirth of the Olympics in 1896, even though running didn't really evolve into a mass participation sport until the early 1970s. A decade into the twenty-first century, running is the world's largest participatory sport and still growing.

Although athletes in the ancient Greek Olympics primarily competed barefoot, specialized footwear for sports existed as far back as the time of the Roman Empire. But it wasn't until the Industrial Revolution that footwear began to evolve, and not until the mid-nineteenth century that specialized running shoes (with spikes for traction) were developed. Materials were generally limited to leather, rubber, wood, nails, yarn, and cloth, and shoes remained fairly primitive until the twentieth century. In the early 1900s, as sport became more of a staple in European and American societies, more companies started to produce shoes for running, although there were far fewer participants than in tennis, soccer, and baseball.

Until the late 1960s running was still primarily an activity of the athletically gifted. There were only a handful of road running races in the United States at the time, and few had as many as 100 participants. However, the rise of the citizen runner was already under way. In addition to increased leisure time and economic stability, the 1960s were also a time of self-expression, pop culture, and individual achievement, each of which played a role in the growth of running among the masses as the decade wore on.

The Rise of Running

When the rise of recreational running began in earnest in the late 1960s, it wasn't born from shoe company marketing campaigns, the desire to achieve a "life-changing accomplishment," or concern about a national obesity epidemic. Certainly people began running for fitness, but those who started the movement were already relatively fit. Many of the participants had run cross-country and track in high school or college and had some base of athleticism, knowledge of training, and experience. Those early adopters of running started training so they could run as fast as possible. Back then, no matter the length of the race, it was that simple. It's no small coincidence that Olympic track and field was seen on TV for the first time in 1960, or that President John F. Kennedy persuaded American citizens to get fit, both by reinvigorating the President's Council on Physical Fitness and with the challenge of running a 50-mile race, the now-famous JFK 50, on the outskirts of Washington, D.C. But at the same time, there was no such thing as using running as a vehicle to raise money for charities and no social status for "just finishing."

One clear indicator of running's slow but measureable increase in popularity is the growth of the Boston Marathon. The oldest marathon in the world, dating back to 1897, it was one of only about a dozen marathons in the United States at the beginning of the 1960s. Although it remained an event for elite runners and serious recreationalists, the country's original marathon grew every single year during the 1960s—from just 197 starters in 1960 to 1,342 by 1969 (BAA n.d.). The New York City Marathon started in 1970 with 127 runners in its first event (NYRR n.d.). Participation was growing there as well, but it didn't start to explode until American icons Frank Shorter and Bill Rodgers burst onto the scene later in the decade.

Fast-forward to the present day and those numbers, impressive at the time, seem impossibly miniscule. In 2009 the New York City Marathon had 43,660 finishers (NYRR n.d.), and a record 467,000 people finished a marathon somewhere in the United States, according to Running USA, an organization that tracks demographic information for the running industry (Running USA 2010). That is a 32 percent increase since 2000 and more than double the number of marathoners in 1990. But until recently, runners have been getting slower and slower. In 1980 the median time for a male marathon finisher in the United States was 3:32; the average women's time was 4:03. By 2002 those numbers had slipped to all-time lows of 4:20 and 4:56, respectively (Running USA 2010).

The reason for this decline is most likely the fact that initially the population of marathon runners was small, and most came from an athletic background and trained with the goal of running a fast time. In the past 25 years, marathons have been crowded with new, untrained runners who are more concerned with finishing than with running fast. But it also has something to do with running mechanics and the shoes people have been training in.

The Shoe Industry Takes Shape

As recreational running began to emerge in the 1960s, so did the running shoe industry. Up to that point, the leading brands had been Onitsuka Tiger from Japan (which later became ASICS) and Adidas from Germany. Both companies were primarily making lightweight shoes for track and field athletes and marathoners, partially because of limitations in materials and manufacturing techniques, but mostly because those are the types of shoes that allow runners to run the best. There is nothing underfoot to inhibit a runner's natural stride, just enough material to provide minimal protection and traction.

Those early shoes were primitive by modern standards, consisting of a semisoft rubber outsole, a thin insole, a firm heel counter, and a nylon upper with an overlaid saddle that when laced created a snug fit in the heel and arch (see Figure 2.1). Most of those shoes had no cushioning, save perhaps for the slight resiliency from the thin rubber outsole, but they offered up just enough underfoot protection to train and race on roads, trails, and cinder tracks without inhibiting the natural flex of a runner's foot or getting in the way of the foot's ability to feel the ground.

Olympic marathoner Frank Shorter remembers the early models well. "The blown rubber was tough. You tended to wear a couple of insoles back then," he says. "You'd put an extra insole in the shoe and were careful about the surfaces you ran on to some extent, but the other point is when you weigh 136 pounds, like I did, you don't need that much. It was being light on the feet that really mattered" (Shorter 2010).

Those flat-soled models were fine for strong, lean, and nimble runners with years of specialized athletic training, but hardly acceptable for the first generation of recreational runners or *joggers*, as they were called in *Jogging*, the 1966 best seller written by University of Oregon track and cross-country coach Bill Bowerman.

The Jogging Generation

When Shorter burst onto the American consciousness by winning the 1972 Olympic marathon in Munich (a race shown on TV across the United States), a multitude of new runners started pounding the pavement as the running boom began in earnest. Shorter returned to take the silver medal in 1976 in Montreal, and Bill Rodgers went on to earn four wins apiece in the New York City and Boston marathons between 1975 and

Figure **2.1** | *Typical 1970s shoe*

1980. These feats provided a massive aftershock that gave anyone who had thought about becoming a runner in the previous years the impetus to finally get started. As those citizen runners competed in 5Ks, 10Ks, and marathons, the running craze became the zeitgeist that defined a generation. Suddenly everyone was rushing out to buy running shoes to find out what it was all about.

The sense of euphoria and personal accomplishment that running provided was contagious, with seemingly unlimited potential for growth. Who wouldn't want to invest in a pair of running shoes and put in some sweat equity by running every day, with the almost-guaranteed return of improved health; increased happiness; and a self-generating, lifelong passion that is easier, cheaper, and more accessible than tennis, bowling, golf, or bicycling?

People took to running because it was easy and generally required no inherent athletic skill. You just needed to lace up the shoes and go. But that kind of oversimplification played a role in the demise of natural running. Although plenty of people were signing up for races and preparing to run a marathon, few were learning how to run or the importance of good form or training.

When this new population of citizen runners complained of everything from mild soreness to debilitating injuries from the minimally designed footwear, shoe companies took note and started to develop footwear specifically for the new phenomenon of jogging, with comfort and cushioning as top priorities. Were those early shoes poorly designed, or were these new citizen runners not dynamically strong and not running with good mechanics? The answer was probably a little of both.

"Back in the 1960s, the only people who were really running were very serious runners. Joe Average was not out there doing it back then," says Charlie Rodgers, co-owner of the Bill Rodgers Running Center in Boston. "There wasn't much to the first running shoes, and only the elite guys were able to really run in them" (Rodgers 2010).

Some of the changes and developments designed to suit this new class of citizen runners were definitely good, but others altered the inherent kinematic process of the human body while running. Initially shoe companies tried to add cushioning by creating outsoles and midsoles from polyurethane, but this added too much weight and was too firm. The biggest breakthroughs came when shoe makers started using ethylene vinyl acetate (EVA)—a dense but soft, elastic, and flexible foam—as the primary cushioning agent (see Figure 2.2). It was a big improvement on earlier models of shoes, but the soft foam also gave a much different sensation underfoot and altered a foot's ability to sense the ground and send feedback to the brain about how the rest of the body should move.

Boston-based New Balance jumped into the running shoe business in the early 1960s with the introduction of the Trackster. One of the first mass-produced shoes built primarily for running, it developed a strong regional following in New England and became the shoe of choice for that first generation of joggers and other fitness buffs. Although it had a thin leather upper and looked like a golf shoe, it had a snug-fitting last (the solid form around which a shoe is built) enhanced by a three-pronged leather saddle that enabled the lacing system to provide midfoot support and a dynamic athletic fit. It had a slightly raised heel, by way of a thin, firm wedge of sloping foam between the rubber outsole and midsole foam.

Other manufacturers, including Nike (cofounded by *Jogging* author Bill Bowerman) and a company owned by famed coach Arthur Lydiard, came up with new ideas and new designs, including the waffle-patterned polyurethane outsole Bowerman originally concocted using his wife's waffle iron. But as soon as shoe designs started to morph, so did the

Figure **2.2** | *A 1970s running shoe with an EVA sole*

running mechanics of joggers. Nike's first jogging shoe, the Cortez, was one of the first to feature a significantly lifted rear heel (created by a dual-density foam wedge), which Bowerman believed would help propel a jogger forward and ease the strain on the Achilles tendon. It was perhaps a logical line of thought at the time, but it negated the necessary action of elastic recoil that plays a central role in allowing a runner to run relaxed with light footsteps. Ultimately it set in motion a trend that would influence running shoe design—and alter and inhibit the natural form of millions of runners—for the next 40 years.

Soaring Sales and Shifting Shoe Design

As the running boom continued gaining momentum through the mid-1970s, running shoes cost between $18 and $50 and were primarily sold at sporting goods and department stores. Back then there was no such thing as a running store. In 1977 the country's two preeminent marathoners—Shorter and Rodgers—independently started two of the first running specialty shops in the world. Even though the stores popped up in different locales—the first of what would become a successful chain of Frank Shorter Sports shops was located on the Pearl Street Mall in the hippie hangout and burgeoning running mecca of Boulder, Colorado, while the Bill Rodgers Running Center settled in historic downtown Boston—each had a similar business model: namely, tapping into the experience of elite runners to sell running shoes and dispense running advice to the growing number of health-oriented joggers and recreational runners.

With record numbers of race participants every year, sales of running shoes were soaring. Adidas and ASICS were still the world leaders, with domestic brands new to the running shoe business, such as Nike, Brooks, Etonic, and Saucony, on the fast track. In 1976 an estimated 3 million pairs of running shoes were sold in the United States, with the Nike Waffle Racer and the New Balance 320 at the top of the heap. At the same time, 25,000 American runners finished a marathon, a huge number compared to the few hundred who covered a 26.2-mile race when the decade started. That number would continue soaring through the end of the decade, reaching 143,000 by 1980.

Running Shoes for Newcomers

By then running shoes had evolved considerably, with most changes aimed at newcomers to the sport. New materials, manufacturing techniques, and an ever-growing consumer base led to frenzied competition among running shoe brands, which in turn influenced design features. With every brand touting the latest and greatest new features in glossy advertisements in new magazines such as *Runner's World*, *The Runner*, and *The Marathoner*, runners were being hit with a blitz of marketing as they decided which new training shoes to purchase. Although many of the changes were performance or comfort oriented, only a few were aimed at preserving the natural motion of the foot, enabling good, economical running form or allowing afferent feedback between the foot and the ground.

Shoe designs were still fairly simple, which helped keep shoes lightweight. But most new models shared two characteristics: They had considerably more EVA foam in the midsole, and virtually all had a lifted heel. By the mid-1970s the heel lift was universally considered the best way to build a training shoe. For nonrunners just entering the sport and perhaps more interested in health and fitness than competition, this design might even have made practical sense. Most recreational runners of the day lacked the dynamic foot, leg, and core strength as well as the good, economical running form of their elite racing contemporaries; those flat-bottomed, lightweight trainers might have sent first-generation joggers running for aspirin, bringing the running boom to a screeching halt.

More Cushioning

Increasingly, cushioning became the most important feature in running shoes. And as manufacturers inserted more foam and different kinds of materials underfoot (especially in the heel, the preferred landing point of new, untrained, and largely inefficient runners) to help absorb the shock of pounding the pavement, a vicious 30-year war among shoe brands was set off. That multibillion-dollar competition—focused on the technology, resiliency, and comfort of midsole cushioning—put companies into a make-or-break battle for survival and created a paradox in the running world: The technological and design advances of each individual company, combined with considerable marketing efforts, helped grow the sport exponentially, and that meant everybody won. But the increased participation only furthered the competition among brands. Suddenly there were thousands of races around the country, and by 1979, 10 million American runners bought pairs of running shoes.

Also in 1979 Nike, which already owned 50 percent of the U.S. market, introduced its first shoes with Air-Sole cushioning technology (durable, sealed pouches of pressurized gas imbedded in the midsole that compressed under impact and then sprang back). The new technology, developed by former aerospace engineer Frank Rudy, was an instant success, pushing Nike further into the lead among running shoe manufacturers and leading other brands to develop softer foams (Saucony Jazz), gel packets (an ASICS cushioning staple for the next 30 years), and other gimmicks (for example, Reebok's semi-inflatable shoe called The Pump) to keep up with Nike's fast-growing promotional machine. The competition and marketing push among brands only increased the industrywide emphasis on soft midsole materials and heel-cushioning technology.

Shoes Move from Functional to Fashionable

As competition among manufacturers continued over the next two decades, shoe brands put more emphasis on aesthetic design, exposed or "visible" technology (designs that allowed consumers to see air bags, gel packets, and various stabilizing, cushioning, and propulsion pieces), and the nebulous concept of "step-in comfort" (a plush feeling customers could sense the moment they tried on a shoe at a retail store). As running shoes became softer, higher off the ground, and heavier, they became less and less conducive to the natural running mechanics still practiced by elite runners and more a lifestyle shoe for commuting to work, walking around the mall, going to the movies, doing errands, mowing the lawn, and even going out on a casual date.

These developments played a key role in taking the focus away from running fast and economically. They ultimately had devastating effects on the running mechanics of two generations of runners, who without proper training or dynamic foot, leg, and core strength; unable to sense the ground in highly cushioned shoes; and having to run in increasingly heavier shoes, didn't have much of a chance to run fast. (There have always been a handful of low-to-the-ground racing flats that are more conducive to natural running. But those shoes have always been marketed to elite runners and not the average runner who walks into a running store looking for a pair of everyday trainers. In addition, racing flats have also morphed through the years, with many having very soft foam and moderate heel-toe ramp angles.)

In the 1980s and 1990s industrial designers working for shoe companies helped make running shoes more fashionable and wearable outside of running. People started wearing running shoes as their everyday casual footwear, both because they were soft and comfortable and because they branded the wearer with the "I'm a runner" status that had become so socially appealing. Suddenly running shoes were an object of pop culture, with glitzy TV commercials that inspired the "Just Do It" generation. But at the same time, some brands lost sight of hardcore runners and the focus on running because there was a lot of revenue coming in from "lifestyle" wearers.

By the early 2000s there were more runners wearing shoes with some kind of stabilizing mechanism than any other kind of shoe (see Figure 2.3). But which came first, the chicken or the egg? Did poor running form cause runners to land with heavy, heel-striking footsteps and overpronate? Or did shoes with built-up heels and thick amounts of midsole cushioning cause runners to have bad mechanics and land with heavy heel-striking footsteps? Maybe the answer is both.

Figure **2.3** | Running shoe circa 2000

One dilemma is that shoe companies haven't always tried to develop the best shoe possible for a particular type of runner; instead, they have tried to develop a shoe to compete with the market leader and other competitors. Making running shoes is a business, and putting a shoe out that looks or acts differently from others on the market is risky. It's difficult for a company to take those kinds of bold chances, but it's easy to put something out that looks similar and claim that it is better, even if there is no quantitative proof. Take, for example, the energy and focus tied to heel technology. For much of the past three decades, "stop overpronation" has been the biggest catchphrase in the running shoe industry. Consequently, much of the so-called technological innovation, marketing pizzazz, and earnest research and development have been focused on the heel of shoes.

Shifting Focus to the Forefoot

I had worked for years with traditional running shoe testing labs around the country. They all had a test centered on the *heel* of footwear. Believe it or not, no test has been established in the American Society for Testing and Materials (ASTM) or international footwear testing groups to measure forces on the forefoot. All modern footwear production revolved around only the testing of heel technology and material properties until Newton came on to the scene. Several testing labs argued that they could modify a heel test to measure these conditions on forefoot technology or foam. Newton Running technology required a test that shifted its focus to the forefoot of the shoe. Ultimately, we began designing tests and understanding what was available and useful forefoot information.

Since 2007 I have had the privilege to work with two classes at the Massachusetts Institute of Technology. Professor Alex Slocum's advanced engineering class asked me to present a problem in my industry that needed to be solved. Naturally, I suggested the class try to develop a test to measure the impact forces, shock-absorbing properties, and energy-return capabilities of the *forefoot* area of running shoes.

The MIT engineering class ended up designing a machine that duplicates impact forces generated by humans running. Measurements taken by a foot structure inside the shoe record data from the surface area of the whole foot. The device also allows the testing shoe to strike at the heel, midfoot, or forefoot and record measurements that are comparable from shoe to shoe. The team demonstrated the proof-of-concept machine they designed, and hopefully it can be embraced by the running industry as a standard test.

Until recently shoe companies have not focused their time and resources on research. They have tried in vain to slow down the rotational forces from heel striking by creating dual-density heel crash pads that soften the blow of the impact and let the foot roll into a harder density medial post. As a result, runners deemed to have a less-than-neutral gait have been put into stability or motion control shoes. But overpronation (the excessive inward rolling motion of the foot) is actually caused by a hard heel-striking gait that makes the foot and ankle a loose adapter, thus making them more vulnerable to rotational forces. Weak feet, ankles, and lower legs, as well as built-up heels in shoes, also contribute to the problem, but the biggest factor is that the considerable impact force of a heel-striking gait accentuates the instability of the ankle. Running with a heel-striking gait isn't natural, but we've been conditioned to think that it is because most shoes have had cushy midsoles and built-up heels. Our brain thinks that it's safe to land on those soft heels, and it's really the only way to strike the ground in those shoes anyway, because the built-up heels get in the way even if you try to run with a midfoot/forefoot gait.

Overpronation or oversupination (which is the excessive outward rolling motion of the foot) isn't an issue when running with light foot strikes under the body mass; in that case, the ankle and rear foot become locked and stable, because the support of the body is maintained by the muscles, bones, and fascia of the forefoot, arch, and flexed knee and don't allow for any significant rolling at the heel.

As mentioned previously, the change in my own running style, which led to plantar fasciitis, made me question whether runners really needed more support and soft cushioning in their running shoes. I surmised then that we didn't need a rigid orthotic focusing on the rear foot, but rather something like the ski insoles that I had made for years to keep skiers balanced and in control of their skis. It seemed to me that most of the in-shoe pronation control measures didn't solve the problem; instead they exacerbated it by inflicting more impact on the foot and lower leg and putting a runner even more out of balance.

Better Science and Better Form

Recent research indicates that trying to slow impact forces by wearing shoes with a lifted heel isn't a smart idea. A study published in the *British Journal of Sports Medicine* suggested that prescribing stability or motion control shoes based on foot type is overly simplistic and likely injurious (Ryan et al. 2010). After 30 years of shoe companies suggesting (or even *dictating*) how we run, people are figuring out that we might have been led astray.

Physical therapist Jay Dicharry, director of the SPEED Performance Clinic at the University of Virginia's Center for Endurance Sport, is also skeptical that shoe companies know what is best for runners. "Companies and running stores have told us for a long time that these dual-density posts are in the heel area to stop or to slow pronation, but peak pronation isn't even happening during heel contact anyway," he says. "I think there's still a big disconnect between the science and the shoes. There's good footwear out there now, but there's still a long way to go" (Dicharry 2009/2010).

Studies have shown that even putting novice runners into comprehensive training programs doesn't reduce the rate of running-related injuries. But that does not mean that cushioned and overly supportive running shoes are the sole culprit. More likely a combination of several things—footwear, a runner's level of fitness and strength, and running mechanics—leads to the continued high injury rates among runners, says Mark Cucuzzella, MD, an associate professor at the West Virginia University Department of Family Medicine and a competitive masters marathoner who has studied running injuries and running form extensively (Cucuzzella 2009/2010).

The bottom line is that different ways of thinking about running form, running shoes, and running in general were bound to emerge as the number of runners continues to grow. "As human beings, we will not come in new and improved models," Cucuzzella says. "The key to running injury-free is to focus on your form first, be strong and stable and get shoes that work with that. After that you can train and the speed will come. But to be a healthy runner, you really have to run naturally with less impact."

New Thinking

Recent programs like ChiRunning, Evolution Running, Radiant Running, Stride Mechanics, and Barefoot Running have espoused some aspects of natural running techniques that include upright posture with a slight forward lean, short strides with a high cadence, and foot striking directly under the hips. Although these programs are similar, there are plenty of not-so-subtle differences, which have become fodder for debate among running biomechanists and on Internet message boards. The problem is that virtually all of these ways of thinking about running form were developed to work with heel-lifted, highly cushioned training shoes or, at the other end of the spectrum, completely unshod feet.

Getting people to recognize their own biomechanical inefficiencies after years of being proficiently inefficient in traditional training shoes can be a challenge, says Toronto-based running coach and form guru Malcolm Balk, author of *Master the Art of Running* (2006). Longtime runners are often set in their ways and don't see the need to change, and new runners find it to be a lot of work, even though small adjustments lead to big improvements.

"As people age, a runner's stride almost becomes a caricature of what it once was," says Balk, who uses the Alexander Technique, a method utilizing good biomechanics and posture awareness in running and other everyday activities. "Chances are they've had some kind of injury at some point or their body has changed or what they do in their daily life has changed, and that's affected their gait, and they've never gone about correcting it. They weren't aware of what they were doing in the first place, and they've never gone through the process of reeducating themselves to develop a better, more sound technique." Having a few extra pounds on the body or sitting in a chair or a vehicle most of the day can also be hurdles.

Mark Cucuzzella's Story

That's exactly where Mark Cucuzzella, a sub-2:30 marathoner, found himself in 2000. After more than 20 years of competitive running, the former University of Virginia track and cross-country competitor started experiencing severe pain in his feet due to arthritis and other degenerative changes. Although he was only 34 at the time and very fit, running was becoming very laborious, painful, and frustrating.

"I figured my days of running pain-free were over," Cucuzzella says (2009/2010). Instead of giving up, he set out to learn about the biomechanics of running. He watched how über-efficient East Africans ran, he watched how barefoot runners ran, and he took special notice of the way he ran. He realized he had become too much of a heel-striker and came across Romanov's Pose Method. One of the first "technique gurus" to preach something other than the status quo was Russian biomechanist and Olympic coach Dr. Nicholas Romanov, who in the mid-1970s developed and started teaching the Pose Method—a running technique that stresses impact reduction and maximizes the use of gravity and momentum. First published in Russian in 1981 and translated into English and made available worldwide in 1997, the method focuses on forefoot striking and the notion that the entire body is suspended by the muscles in the calf. Using a body position similar to that of a sprinter, a Pose runner maintains forward momentum by utilizing gravity with a dramatically forward-leaning posture.

Cucuzzella retooled his running form with a lower-impact midfoot gait and started to feel improvements. But it wasn't until 2005, when he read Danny Dreyer's *ChiRunning*, a program centered on a holistic approach to running technique utilizing tenets of the Chinese martial art of tai chi, that Cucuzzella started to put it all together: deriving power from his core and running with a high cadence, short strides, foot strikes under his hips, and an upright posture.

"You have to look at the whole mechanics of the movement," he says. "You can't just say, 'I'll try to land on my midfoot,' because it's much more than that. It's about how the whole process fits together. Learning all of the principles and continually improving is important."

Cucuzzella's personal breakthroughs made him want to share what he learned with others. Combining his medical training with his passion for running, he delved into the topic in 2007 by surveying 2,500 people who had bought Dreyer's book; he found, among other things, that participants reported a 30 percent reduction in injuries and a 40 percent reduction in perceived discomfort over six-month periods (Cucuzzella and West Virginia University 2007).

"Up until recently, if you were running and your knee hurts, you go to the doctor, you get an MRI or you take some ibuprofen or you stop running," Cucuzzella says. "But we need to think about why we're hurt."

He recently followed up his study by putting 20 marathoners through a running form workshop, the primary tenet of which was running with efficient mechanics that included foot strikes at the midfoot. His goal was to be able to go beyond the conceptual evidence and testimonial results and advance the field of study.

"As a doctor, I want to keep people healthy," Cucuzzella says. "From my perspective, we've made zero progress in preventing and treating running injuries. People still get hurt at the same rate—40 to 60 percent a year—despite the MRIs and all of the care they get now. We need to find better ways—as runners, coaches, doctors and the shoe industry."

With his work on his form, Cucuzzella's running has been revitalized and virtually pain-free, although he admits he's slowed down slightly as he's gotten older. In 2008 he clocked a 2:34 at the Boston Marathon (14th masters finisher) and Marine Corps Marathon (1st masters finisher) and then won the masters division (11th overall) at the JFK 50 Mile with a new PR of 6:45:48.

Now he feels that he can run at a high level forever, thanks mainly to his revamped style of running, which allows him to significantly reduce his recovery time. At age 44 he ran the 2010 Boston Marathon in 2:34:21, which was good enough for a 10th-place finish among masters (age 40 and over) runners.

The Industry Takes a Minimalist Approach

Although natural running is about efficient mechanics and balanced-with-gravity posture, it also requires shoes with specific design criteria. Most natural and midfoot running stride proponents recommend light-weight footwear that mimics a barefoot stride. Shoes with a level profile and firm materials under the midfoot/forefoot—as opposed to those with a soft, cushy midsole and a large heel crash pad—allow a runner to land with flat foot strikes at the midfoot and develop the proprioception necessary for efficient running, while also allowing for the natural settling of the heel after the initial impact of the foot to enable the energy return of elastic recoil before a new stride begins.

"You need to feel the road," says Dreyer, a renowned running instructor. "The more your feet can really feel the ground, the more it will educate the rest of your body on how to move and how to run" (Dreyer 2009).

Finally, Research Support

Nike was the first to jump into the natural running game with a commercial product, releasing the first of several models of its Free shoes in 2004. The $2.1 billion running shoe brand took cues from the small but effective amounts of barefoot running that then-Stanford coach Vin Lananna had been putting his distance running charges through. Nike launched a comprehensive study of barefoot biomechanics with a goal of learning as much as possible about barefoot running and using that knowledge to design a minimalist shoe that would enable natural running mechanics. The company devised an über-flexible shoe that allowed the foot to flex and move as it might while barefoot (although critics point out that it still has a very soft and foamy feeling underfoot and includes a lifted heel).

In 2009 and 2010 three independent research studies confirmed the notion that people run differently barefoot than they do while wearing shoes (Kerrigan et al. 2009; Lieberman et al. 2010; Squadrone and Gallozzi 2010). Each also praised the benefits of barefoot running and uninhibited natural running form—namely having foot strikes at the midfoot under a person's center of mass, less impact on the body, and better all-body kinematics—while offering numerous caveats about safety, duration, transition, and a runner's personal history.

"It's essentially a way of running in which the impacts from the collision with the ground are much less perceptible," says Daniel Lieberman, the Harvard evolutionary biologist who concluded in a 2010 study that running with midfoot foot strikes, either barefoot or in shoes, is better and has less impact than heel striking. "That's why you can run barefoot and that's why people ran barefoot before modern running shoes were invented. There wasn't all that cushion and all of that stuff [in the midsole of a shoe] that made the impact transients comfortable."

Furthermore, as of 2010 a dozen brands were selling or working on shoes aimed at midfoot or natural running gaits, including my own Newton Running, as well as Nike, Vibram, Karhu, Ecco, ASICS, New Balance, K-Swiss, Merrell, Saucony, and Terra Plana. The trend is finally taking off at retail shops which, understandably given the 30 percent annual growth of running shoe sales, had been locked into the status quo of the industry for years. This is all evidence that points to the natural running revolution taking off in earnest. But why now?

Retailers as Health Consultants

Mainstream news outlets, the best-selling *Born to Run*, and innumerable Internet blogs have sparked the revolution. The more people know, the more they want to know, especially athletes, who are a particularly hungry audience, always eager for the newest and latest information. Increasingly they are turning to running shops for insight and advice about injuries, preventative treatments, and training. Running shoe retailers have their fingers on the pulse of what ails Americans, at least the active ones among us. For example, in addition to determining what kind of foot type and running mechanics a customer has, Kris Hartner and his staffers at the Naperville Running Company in suburban Chicago make it a point to get to know their customers as runners: the amount of mileage they put in, the type of training they're doing, their personal best times, races they might be training for, and current or previous injuries or niggles they may have. That can get pretty personal, but most customers love it because they know it will help them find the best shoe for their needs.

Sometimes a quick check of wear patterns on the bottom of a training shoe can tell volumes about what's going on with a runner's gait, what kind of discomfort that person is suffering, or how the runner may be compensating biomechanically for a chronic injury. Sure, the shoe store is still selling shoes, even if the staff member is talking about overhauling a new runner's gait or tweaking the form of someone who has been running for 20 years. But the retailer is also acting as running-oriented health consultant.

"I used to be a guy who would say 'you run how you run, don't mess with it,' and I guess it was kind of a lazy man's answer. But when it comes down to it, no, that's absolutely not true," says Hartner, a competitive masters runner whose shop was named the No. 1 running retail store in the U.S. in 2009. "I think most people can probably benefit from working on their form and landing on the ground properly. After getting to know them and their running, we try to offer insights that might help them become more efficient. And the beauty of it is that you can help people a lot in less than a minute" (Hartner 2009/2010).

It's that simple, and it's how a running re-evolution begins.

3

Into the Lab

Examining Your Running Form

Better running begins with your form. I don't mean what you *think* you know about yourself and how you run, or how you've *seen* other good runners run. I'm talking about the biomechanics of how you stand and run right now, no matter what kind of fitness or experience you have.

You might think that running form really only matters to elite runners. That's a bad assumption. In fact, good running mechanics and minor form improvements are arguably more important for recreational runners and their faster, more serious subset, competitive age-groupers. Although highly trained elite runners are so fine-tuned that shaving just a few seconds off their time is considered a big success, a recreational athlete can drop large chunks of time off a personal best marathon time by becoming a stronger and more efficient runner. So whether you've run a 3:10 or 3:45 marathon, with a little bit of work and focus on natural running, you might be within reach of getting below the lofty plateaus of 3:00 or 3:30. Improving your form might be the difference between reaching your time goal or finally reaching your age-group qualifying time for the Boston Marathon.

Think about your body as if it were a car. What if you put four new tires on your car but didn't fix the alignment? Not only would your car lack the handling performance while moving in traffic or turning a corner, but the tires would show inconsistent wear patterns and might contribute to lower gas mileage. The same thing applies to your body when you put shoes on. You must check your alignment—in other words, your posture and running mechanics— to become most efficient.

Ultimately, running with good, efficient form allows you to run with optimal running economy. If you have a small or large form deficiency, you're forcing your body (or your engine) to work harder to process oxygen and pump it through your bloodstream than if you were running at the same pace with more efficient form.

Test out the importance of form for yourself. Run a lap around a track or at a local park with your hands held behind your back. You will feel your heart beating harder than during a normal run because your body lacks the forward propulsion assistance from an alternating arm swing. You can verify this by wearing a heart rate monitor. After warming up with a jog of a mile or so, run that 400-meter lap around a track or any predetermined loop while keeping an eye on your heart rate at the halfway mark and the finish. Then run the same pace with your arms behind your back or your hands on your head and note your heart rate at the halfway mark and the finish. Your heart rate will likely be 10 to 20 percent higher for that same short period of running.

That's an extreme example. You wouldn't knowingly run with your arms behind your back during a training run or a race. You don't purposely run with minor or major form flaws either, yet it still happens. And although those kinds of form deficiencies might not cause a 10 to 20 percent spike in your heart rate, they can certainly make your heart work harder, by 1 to 5 percent on a training run or during a 10K, half-marathon, or marathon. Think of the impact that might have midway through the race you trained so hard for over the previous months. If you're already operating at a few percentage points below your optimal running economy and thus working harder than you should be, what do you think will happen when your body fatigues and those form deficiencies become more pronounced? Ultimately your body is going to have to work even harder. So if you're shooting for a 40-minute 10K or a 1:45

half-marathon or a 3:15 marathon (or any time goal for any race), you'll be giving up valuable time with every single stride and compromising your ability to reach your goal.

The key to optimal form is being in a position that allows you to be balanced with gravity and strong enough and fit enough to maintain it for 1 to 4 hours, or however long your run or race might be. For some runners, that might entail starting from scratch and forgetting everything you know (or never knew) about running, whereas for others it might be eliminating a few bad habits. Whether you have just started running in the last few years or have been running for a long time, you might need to relearn (or learn for the first time) how to run properly, break bad habits, and then build strength and do the proper exercises. Chances are you were never taught how to run. The good news is that you can start today and put yourself on the path to becoming a stronger, more efficient natural runner. Start with examining your body and your structural mechanics and determining how you stand, how you move, and eventually how you run. I call this "pre-hab"—getting to a starting position where you are balanced with gravity, neutral in alignment, and mostly symmetrical in your movements.

Ultimately, good, efficient form leads to less impact and minimal rotational forces, which equals healthier, less impactful running. And that leads to more enjoyment, better fitness, and even faster race times.

How Do *You* Run?

Like snowflakes, everyone's running form is different. Take time to observe the people you run with regularly or watch a few runners the next time you run a 10K or marathon. Some runners might look pretty smooth and comfortable, while others look downright uncomfortable and even pained. Dramatic form flaws are easy to spot. You might see some people leaning to one side. Someone might have one arm that flails out. You're bound to see someone tilting her head to the left or right, and a few might run with an asymmetrical pattern of alternately bouncing and scuffing off the ground. Some runners are severe overpronators (their ankles roll significantly inward) or supinators (their ankles roll significantly outward). It's likely that many of those visible form flaws are caused by subtle deficiencies, within the foot or as a result of the way the foot interacts with the ground, that you can't immediately detect. Even runners who look smooth are likely to have an area in which they can improve. You might not be able to detect anything from a quick glance, but a runner might have a subtle or acute pain that crops up during the latter miles of a race or might wind up uncomfortably sore in one specific area of his body.

Running is simple, but it's not as simple as putting one leg in front of the other without any thought or technique to follow. Just running "however you run" would be like swinging a golf club without any training or adherence to proper form. You might be able to hit the ball, but you're likely to be inconsistent and finish with mediocre results after 18 holes.

Whether you're going slowly or fast, jogging or racing, it takes a sophisticated blend of movements to run efficiently. This is called *whole-body kinematics*, a process of your brain positioning your body efficiently and effectively based on the sensory feedback it gets from your forefoot's interaction with the ground (discussed in more detail in Chapter 6). That might sound like a complicated process, but it's not. It's simple and natural, but it does take some reconditioning and learning how to run properly as well as overcoming some small physical circumstances or irregularities we're born with or that we have created through bad habits or daily life.

An irregularity might be something as small and virtually unnoticeable as a raised first metatarsal joint or something very noticeable, like a hypermobile ankle joint that begins the domino effect, throwing a runner's ability to be dynamically balanced with gravity out of whack . . . causing the left foot to pronate . . . , which causes the lower left leg to twist inward and the patellar tendon to track out of line . . . , which forces the left leg muscles and hip flexor of that leg to overwork . . . , which results in more movement in the hips and pelvis . . . , which causes the lower back muscles to work harder . . . , which throws the upper torso out of alignment . . . , which causes the right arm to swing out wider and the head to tilt to the right to try to help the body maintain some semblance of balance. Or you might have so greatly deconditioned the muscles in your feet after years of wearing stiff dress shoes or sturdy boots with a raised heel that your feet and ankles are prone to instability.

These problems can quickly add up to inefficiency, pain, and injury, making running unpleasant at best and even permanently sidelining your training.

High-Tech Help for Your Form

Determining what kind of running form deficiencies you have, where they originate, and how to improve them is not as difficult as you may think and is well worth the effort. In the late 1990s many running shops started doing rudimentary gait analyses by putting customers on a treadmill and videotaping their stride. Although that's a good start, there are a few flaws in that process. First, many shops have runners do that test in shoes, which means any analysis of a runner's gait is based on how that particular shoe's design geometry affects that gait. It might be possible to determine if a runner is overpronating or supinating by watching the video in slow motion, but the excessive rotation might be caused by the shoes and then accentuated by the treadmill. That's why looking at a foot's movement from the rear view isn't very helpful. If those shoes have a 12–18mm lift in the heel and are softly cushioned, neutral shoes, they're very likely to create excessive rotation when the runner's foot lands on the conveyor belt.

Doing the treadmill test barefoot might seem like a better approach; however, the belts of most commercial treadmills are too slack to determine much about a gait pattern. Running on a loose surface like that doesn't closely replicate any natural or unnatural surface that your body is used to running on, so the way your foot strikes and the rest of your kinematics are bound to be affected. In addition, all of this is rendered irrelevant if a shoe salesperson is just trying to fit you into a traditional training shoe with a steep heel-toe ramp angle and some type of hard foam or plastic midsole insert aimed at slowing the rate of those harmful overrotations. Watching someone run with a heel-striking gait in shoes with a high heel lift merely accentuates the rear foot paradigm—that heel striking does, in fact, cause rotational forces—thus verifying that a person needs to wear one of the stability or motion control shoes sold at that store. Instead, the best use of this kind of treadmill session would be to have someone observe your stride from a side view to determine if you are overstriding or your foot strikes are under your center of mass.

The science and study of running mechanics is relatively young and still evolving with technology. Laboratories at the University of Virginia, the University of Delaware, and the University of Calgary, among others, offer state-of-the-art data collection and analysis through the use of high-speed cameras and force plate treadmills. The lab at the SPEED Performance Clinic at the University of Virginia's Center for Endurance Sport is open to the public for a $300 fee, but going there might not be an option for most people. Physical therapist Jay Dicharry, the director of the lab, has examined thousands of runners over the past several years, from new runners to national and international medalists. If you make an appointment at his lab, he'll talk with you about what is bothering you, ask about your running history and current training, and find out what kinds of supplemental exercises and stretching you're doing. Then he'll put you on a $750,000 state-of-the-art treadmill that records the impact force of each of your footsteps. Combined with a series of high-speed cameras that record the positioning of various body parts 500 times per second, the lab records enough detailed data about joint angles; hip, leg, knee, and ankle rotation; and foot-to-ground impact for Dicharry to understand specifically how your body is moving and where it might be out of alignment or weaker than it should be. Using that information, as well as the symptoms you might have noticed, he recommends exercises to help build strength in those areas and improve your mechanics to get you back on the path to being a healthy runner. Dicharry is a big proponent of natural running form and believes the most important aspect of good form is to make sure your foot strikes occur under your center of mass to minimize braking forces and the impact.

The University of Virginia lab draws runners from around the country interested in getting their injuries and form flaws properly diagnosed. This shows the lengths to which committed runners will go to make sure they can run efficiently and healthily, but this might not be the most convenient or cost-effective option for you. However, you can get a quick and simple look at your own form by examining your balance and alignment with a few simple drills.

Determining Your Running Form

Knowing your own particular weaknesses, bad habits, and physical irregularities is a first step to establishing good running form. You may be exhibiting problematic traits you are not even aware of, which crop up particularly during a race or a long run when your body has fatigued.

Self-Analysis

Standing barefoot in front of a mirror on a hard surface will give you a good indication of what parts of your body might be out of alignment. Your hips might be tilted forward, your pelvis might be canted to the left or right, your shoulders might not be level, and your head might be leaning slightly to one side or the other. Those imbalances could be caused by various forefoot abnormalities or a leg-length discrepancy, but no matter how minor, they are accentuated when you run.

Look for telltale signs that suggest that your form needs a makeover. Red flags might range from residual soreness on one side of your body to definitive pain in an ankle or knee joint. There may be no signs at all, yet you still might be slightly to woefully inefficient every time you run, even if you're fit and running fast. It's quite possible to run fast and set a new PR with form deficiencies or even openly bad form, but think of how much faster and more efficient you could be without all of that going on.

Postural Check

Good running posture is good basic posture. To get a glimpse of your own posture, stand in front of a mirror and see how well aligned you are.

Is your head level?

Are your shoulders level?

Are your hips level?

Are your knees facing forward?

Are your feet pointing forward?

Next, stand barefoot in front of the mirror and lift your right leg off the floor (see Figures 3.1a and 3.1b). Begin a slow, deep knee bend on the left leg and watch the line of your hips. Does your pelvis twist out of horizontal balance? If your hip drops hard toward your right (lifted) leg, it means you're likely starting to pronate with the left foot and ankle. That might mean you need to strengthen your left foot, ankle, and hip while also balancing your forefoot with a lightweight, minimally posted orthotic insole. Reverse your stance with your right leg on the ground and your left leg lifted and repeat the drill. You might or might not have the same drop in your hips as you did on the other leg.

If you have experienced muscular soreness or pain predominantly on one side of your body, it might be an indication that you're imbalanced on that foot. You might have an imbalance in your foot that causes a functional leg-length discrepancy, weak adductors, or a weak hip flexor on that side. Later you might start suffering from a chronically tight left iliotibial band because your body began to compensate to avoid the original problem. But that's part of the problem with trying to self-diagnose injuries or visiting a medical professional who isn't keen to see how you run. A secondary injury or annoyance might bother you most—such as the sore IT band—but really it was a forefoot imbalance, a leg-length imbalance, or a weak core that caused that situation.

You might require a lift under your forefoot to get you into a more balanced position while standing, perhaps something as small as a 2–3mm lift, as is the case with two-time Ironman champion Craig Alexander. That seems like an almost insignificant amount, but the lack of it could be wreaking havoc on your running form.

One-Legged Stance Drill

You can get an idea of the tendencies of your running gait by doing a one-legged drill. Standing in front of a mirror, balance on one foot and slowly flex forward at the knee.

Does the ankle of your foot on the ground rotate inward or outward?

Does the knee on that same side rotate?

Do your hips drop forward or to one side?

Do you pull up your shoulders as you dip downward?

Is your head level or tipped forward, backward, or to one side?

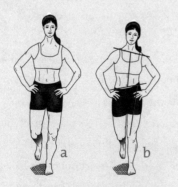

Figure 3.1 | a One-legged stance, healthy
b One-legged stance, off-balance

Running long distances on hard, repetitive surfaces while being out of balance is one of the major causes of overuse injuries.

You can connect almost every overuse injury to the excessive braking/impact and rotational movement or to the excessive force caused by improperly pushing off to begin a new stride, especially if you're starting from an unnatural position. Rotational forces are increased by overstriding and heel striking and typically lead to overuse injuries such as medial knee injuries, a tight iliotibial band, and shin splits, as well as overused braking muscles. Excessive propulsion can create problematically tight hamstrings, Achilles tendons, and connective tissue in the lower leg, ankle, and foot (such as the plantar fascia). I examine these forces more closely in Chapter 7.

Seek Professional Help

If you have had significant discomfort or pain in any part of your body or sense that you might have a form flaw, consider seeking out a professional trained in the biomechanics of the foot and running form. A traditionally trained physical therapist or doctor can be helpful, but unless that person is aware of the specific movements of a running gait and the importance of forefoot balance, chances are you won't receive the precise help you need. As I have said, with running injuries, often it's not what's bothering you that is the actual problem. Someone versed in the specific actions of a running gait should ask questions about your running history and what minor and major aches and pains you are experiencing.

If you came into my running lab and retail shop, I would take you through the same multistep process that I have taken thousands of elite and recreational runners through since 1988. The first thing I do is have a runner stand still and upright in front of me and do a one-legged stance drill so I can analyze her body posture and how she finds a balance with gravity. A person with strong, symmetrical feet and virtually no variables that challenge the ability to find a centered balance will balance on her heels and metatarsal heads and stand up tall with a straight back and level hips and shoulders. Her toes will be relaxed and touching the ground with little pressure, and her legs, hips, shoulders, and head will be vertically and horizontally aligned.

Next, I'd take that person outside and have her run on the sidewalk to observe how her form looks when running. Assuming the runner is balanced and has good mechanics, I will see a symmetrical balance in foot, ankle, and leg movement, as well as symmetrical movements in a compact arm swing.

But in reality, that's not what I see in most people. Running lots of miles for many years (especially in heavily cushioned or supportive shoes with high heel lifts), aging, injuries, and other anatomical variables can result in slight to significant imbalances. And the fact is, we tend to lose muscle and gain fat as we age. Face it, we're just not as slim and strong at 30, 40, 50, or 60 as we were when we were 20. And if you have suffered a minor or major injury that has interrupted your training and required significant rehabilitation, you are not going to run exactly as you did prior to that injury until you rebuild muscle that atrophied during your downtime.

Also, how you spend your time when you're not running could lead to changes in your running form. For example, if you work at a desk and spend 40 hours a week sitting in a chair, this could change your running posture. The same thing applies if you work at a job that requires you to stand for long periods or if you sleep on a very soft mattress. In each case, your body will naturally adjust and compensate to find the necessary position to be balanced with gravity. But because sitting in a chair with a supportive back or arm rests doesn't require the same dynamic muscle interaction as standing or running, you're bound to wind up with a different muscular makeup—especially if you're not doing supplemental core strength work on a regular basis.

All this may sound a little bit overwhelming, maybe even intimidating, and it might be easy to write off minor or major detractions to your form by saying, "Hey, that's just the way I run," or "I'm a natural heel-striker." You can probably point to any number of runners who are better than you with similar or worse problems, from the guy in your running club who runs a minute faster than you in a 10K to Bernard Lagat, the 2007 1,500m and 5,000m world champion and two-time Olympic medalist whose form is often less than fluid. You might watch elite runners in

Form Flaws

Most runners have form flaws, but some are easier to detect than others. Here are a few telltale signs of things you might need to correct.

Are you a loud runner?

You're likely overstriding and hitting the ground on your heel with too much impact. You might even be hitting the ground with a double-impact: First you land hard on your heel, then your forefoot flings forward and slaps the ground with considerable force.

Are you a bouncy runner?

This is a sign that you're heel striking and significantly overstriding. By significantly braking with every heel-strike and then accelerating by pushing off to start a new stride, you're continually raising and lowering your center of mass. If you were to plot the position of your hips on a side view over several strides, you'd see a jagged line with many peaks and valleys. That's not an efficient way to run because you're constantly stopping your momentum, spending more time on the ground than necessary, and using too much muscle energy to start a new stride.

Do you look down in front of you when you run?

If you do, you might be throwing off your center of mass and thus forcing another part of your body to compensate. Your head is a very heavy part of your body, but your body can naturally balance it without too much muscle energy if it's upright. However, leaning your head forward (or to one side) when you run requires considerably more energy to sustain and throws your balance (and your gait pattern) out of whack.

Do you twist your arms, shoulders, and upper body excessively when you run?

In theory, your upper torso and shoulders should be mostly still and upright, while your arms are alternately moving from front to back in the sagittal plane parallel to your body. The more your arms swing across your body (in the coronal plane), the less efficient you'll be. Your arm swing helps you maintain your forward momentum during your running gait, and if your arms are crossing your body and your torso and shoulders are twisting, you're not maximizing that momentum because your energy is being wasted with side-to-side motion.

Can you see your foot landing in front of your body when you look down?

If you look down in the middle of your stride and see your feet landing in front of your body, it means you're overstriding. And if you're overstriding, you're running with an inefficient heel-striking gait.

the lead pack of the Boston Marathon or on the track at the Olympics, or even the better runners in a 10K race in your town, and wonder why they have minor or sometimes even major form flaws. For one thing, running talent—the dynamic combination that might include aerobic capacity and efficiency, dynamic strength, and considerable mental fortitude—can trump form deficiencies to some extent. So if a top-tier runner clocks a 2:06-something and places in the top three at the Chicago Marathon despite a visible form flaw, does that mean he could probably be more efficient and run faster? Probably, but most elite runners are continually working to maintain or improve their running mechanics by doing form drills and exercises to build dynamic functional strength. Any top-level runner you can name—from Deena Kastor, Ryan Hall, and Kara Goucher to Paula Radcliffe, Meb Keflezighi, and Haile Gebrselassie—works on drills and strength exercises to maximize the ability to run efficiently and overcome minor mechanical flaws. (I'll show you how to do those same exercises elsewhere in this book.) The point is, despite some recurring form flaws, those elite athletes have probably already done plenty to improve their mechanics to get to where they are, but to be fair, their incredible cardiovascular abilities help overcome any minor form flaws. However, for every top-tier elite runner, there are thousands of near-elite runners who don't have the cardiovascular system or mechanical efficiency to run with the lead pack.

You might run for a lot of reasons: overall mental and physical health, to run fast race times, or just to finish your first marathon. If you run a new personal best time in a 10K or marathon, you probably think you're running pretty well. But if you want to run your fastest and avoid overuse injuries, you need to run with efficient, natural running form. It's that simple.

Now that you have an idea why good form is important and understand that yours might need work, in Chapter 4 I discuss the science of motion and why natural form is the best way to run.

4

The Science of Motion
Three Gaits

The human body is a wonderfully complex mechanism. Think of all the unique and dynamic ways we can move in any and all directions. We can walk in an upright position. We can jog, run, and sprint. We can move side to side. We can crawl, hop, skip, jump, and lunge. We can spin, roll, somersault, cartwheel, and perform an almost unlimited number of acrobatic moves, assuming we're physically trained, fit, and dexterous enough to pull them off. Furthermore, we can make all those movements very fast, very slow, or somewhere in between. We can move forward, backward, sideways, or diagonally. We can even force our bodies into ill-advised, off-balance movements, and they will always try to find a way to stabilize with gravity. Think about some of the things gymnasts, ballet dancers, and trapeze artists do. Short of flying, there isn't much we can't do. Our only real limit is gravity, the force that keeps us connected to the ground between various movements we consciously (and unconsciously) make.

As runners, it's important to understand our ability to move dynamically, because our bodies seek the best and most natural way to accommodate those movements while interacting with gravity and the surface beneath us. To fully understand how we run with shoes, we have to understand how we run naturally without shoes on a given surface. Barefoot running as a training tool is addressed in Chapter 9, but this chapter discusses running barefoot as it relates to the basic tenets of natural running.

Let's begin by examining how the human body interacts with gravity. To even stand on two feet requires the firing of muscles on the front and back of the legs (braking and propulsive muscles) to balance our entire body mass over the center of our feet in accordance with the downward push from gravity. It all starts with the feet, which first sense the ground and help our brain orchestrate the balancing act and then perform like a dynamic tripod in helping us reach that balance. This is made possible through a sophisticated communication between the foot and the brain, facilitated by the body's vast nervous system (see Figures 4.1 and 4.2).

The feet are complex works of art, and no two, even your own two, are the same. Most feet are naturally positioned level to the ground surface and rely on ground-engaging bones—the heel, forefoot, and toes—to achieve that all-body balance. (I address what happens when feet aren't naturally positioned level to the ground in Chapter 5.)

Before the brain can begin the balancing act, it needs to understand details about the surface beneath your feet. The bottoms of your feet are much more sensitive than your hands, and that makes sense if you consider that the feet serve as the primary balancing mechanism for the entire body. That's a big responsibility, and it's why there is such a highly sophisticated network of cutaneous receptors in the forefoot region of the foot (or the ball of the foot area) under your metatarsal heads.

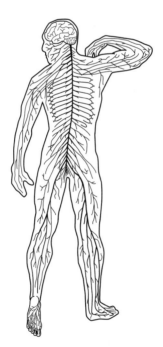

Figure **4.1** | *The brain and body are connected via a vast network of nerves.*

The brain takes sensory information from your feet to the central nervous system to instantly communicate and react to stimuli. Slowly walk or jog barefoot across any surface without looking at the ground, and you will be amazed at what your feet communicate to your brain. Is the surface hot or cold? Is it smooth and stable or rough and unstable? Hard or soft? Wet or dry? The feedback from these ground-engaging sensors of the feet triggers the whole body to respond to what is happening under the foot. In other words, the body reacts to the specific details of what is sensed under the foot and positions and moves it accordingly.

The whole body reacts to initial movement—the head, shoulders, arms, spine, hips, legs, and feet. This amazing balancing act allows us to move with our entire bodies to stay upright and deal with gravity. This beautiful human movement is a giant action and equal opposite reaction. For example, if you step on a small pebble while walking barefoot on a sidewalk, you quickly lift that foot off the ground to stop the irritating pain stimulus it sensed. As you do so, your entire body reacts to recenter and rebalance itself with gravity. Depending on how abruptly you react, your arms might flail a bit to help offset the quick, reactionary movement of your foot, leg, and hips. If your other foot lands on a smooth, stable surface, the body stops moving so vigorously, and you settle into a balancing position. If you were to hop

Figure 4.2 | *Nervous system, foot*

onto your other foot and land on a small pebble, you'd immediately hop off that foot and back to the original as your body continued to seek out an ideal balance with gravity.

This is possible because feet are highly complex and have the ability to brake and adapt, stabilize, lock, lever, and propel. They can adjust to variations of surfaces and articulations that allow for essentially three different gaits: the walking gait (heel-strikes), running gait (midfoot strikes), and sprinting gait (toe strikes).

Knowing the differences among the three gait styles is one of the lynch-pins of understanding and the first step in the transition to better, more efficient running mechanics. There has been plenty of debate about the gait styles used by runners, but numerous recent research studies and many doctors, physical therapists, coaches, and runners concur that there are distinct gaits for each of those speeds of forward movement. For reasons I explain below, the body is just not set up to run with a walking gait.

Let's look more closely at the walking, running, and sprinting gaits and our foot and whole body positions during these movements, without footwear and on a natural surface.

Walking Gait

Walking is extremely efficient. With proper nutrition and hydration, we could walk for days if we needed to. There is very little impact on the body while walking because of the slower speed of the movement. We lever more from the hip area, which creates a long but slow, efficient lever arm for forward momentum.

Without delving into the many micromovements of the walking gait cycle, let's focus on the three main points of contact with the foot plant and body position during walking: heel-strike, mid-stance, and toe-off.

When you're walking, you're moving at a slow to moderate speed and continually braking and adapting (heel-strike; see Figure 4.3a) with your heel, coming to a neutral-with-gravity centered position (mid-stance; see Figure 4.3b) that allows your opposite foot to push off the ground behind you (toe-off; see Figure 4.3c) and start cycling through a new stride as your body rolls forward. When the foot that was originally forward and then

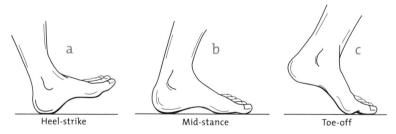

| Heel-strike | Mid-stance | Toe-off |

Figure **4.3** │ *Walking gait*

at mid-stance is behind your center of mass, you enact a slight muscular force to push off and begin a new stride.

As we analyze the three phases, it becomes clear what the functions of the foot and upper body are and how they are optimized when we walk, run, and sprint.

Phase One: Heel-Strike

In heel-strike the mechanics of the rear foot (heel bone and ankle system) are in a braking and adaptive mode, and the extended leg and foot are in front of the body mass. The foot is a "loose adapter," meaning the ankle can either pronate or supinate to adapt to changing surfaces the body is moving over. In this phase, the ankle is the great adapter for all terrain, meaning when the heel strikes the ground first while walking, it will adapt to variations of the surface underfoot. The heel touches the ground in front of the body, creating a braking and adapting effect before the next phase.

Phase Two: Mid-Stance

At mid-stance, the upper body is centered over the midfoot and balanced with gravity, and the foot is stable and locked, now ready for the toe-off phase.

Phase Three: Toe-Off

At toe-off, the foot is in a levering and propulsive position. The upper body mass is now forward of the toeing-off foot, and the body is moving forward.

A Closer Look at Heel-Strike and Toe-Off

Heel striking is braking and adapting and is used in the walking gait, in which the body takes very little impact and uses the legs and hips to lever the body efficiently forward for miles or days at a time. The foot is on the ground for the longest amount of time and has the largest amount of surface area in contact with the ground. It's a process of braking, adapting, locking, levering, and propelling.

The lower body isolates braking muscles and then uses propulsive muscles to walk forward. Because of the slower speed of walking, there is very little impact force to deal with, and the use of both braking and propulsive muscles is minimal. That's very efficient for walking speeds.

As mentioned previously, in the toe-off phase the foot is ready to be used as a propulsive lever. Isn't this how we sprint? When we sprint, we are way up on the front of the metatarsals and toes to leverage as much speed and power as possible from the foot and propulsive muscles and tendons located in the back of the legs. The upper body mass is slightly ahead of or directly over the foot landing. In direct opposition to the walking gait, as you sprint your foot is on the ground for the least amount of time, and the least amount of surface area is contacting. By landing way up on the toes and metatarsals, the body activates only propulsive muscles and connective tissue.

Sprinting is a flight mechanism, and we can only sustain sprinting in short bursts. Sprinting is running very fast with maximal power from 20 yards to 400 meters, but it is a very inefficient use of energy. It uses a great amount of muscle energy and forces the heart and lungs to work at levels that cannot be sustained for very long. Yet the foot and body position described above is still the most efficient and effective for generating maximum speed and power, albeit for short distances.

A Closer Look at Mid-Stance

Figure 4.3a shows where you land when you walk, and Figure 4.3c portrays where you land when you sprint. Figure 4.3b, mid-stance, shows where you want to apply your foot to the ground *while running*.

Running is not the walking gait, nor is it the sprinting gait. Running is landing at your midfoot/forefoot, parallel to the ground surface. The ball of the foot first touches lightly to sense the surface, then the rest of the foot settles downward to touch the ground lightly. This foot strike and subsequent settling of the heel initiate elastic recoil, our body's ability to spring back energy from muscle and tendon. In other words, it resets our foot and leg and prepares it for the next stride. As the upper body moves forward and the foot starts to lever, a simple lift of the foot off the ground occurs. Essentially, running, or at least the way your body is inclined to do it naturally, is a series of one-legged stances landing under the center of your mass.

The next section breaks down the running gait in greater detail.

Running Gait

The greatest differences between a running and walking gait are that motions of the body are quicker and there is a higher stride cadence when running. (See Figures 4.4a, 4.4b, and 4.4c.) Because of that, you have to start a new stride immediately after a foot touches the ground. To do that, your upper body needs to remain in an upright, slightly forward-leaning posture to maintain momentum.

Most people actually run with a heel-striking walking gait, not realizing the many negative effects that has on running form, efficiency, and economy. Running with a walking gait foot strike results in overstriding, increased braking/impact and rotational forces, a slow cadence because of the extended time spent from the heel-strike and mid-stance phases, and the need for enormous muscular force to push off the ground to keep momentum going and begin a new stride.

Running with a walking gait creates a vicious and inefficient cycle from which you can't recover. You're always playing catch-up because your planted foot is always on the ground longer, thus making it harder to increase your cadence. That requires more muscular force to start a new stride and keep the upper body moving, and you're suddenly back in the same position you were on the previous stride. Sure, you can run a marathon with a walking gait, but it's far from the most efficient way to run.

The way to eliminate this unproductive cycle is to make your foot strikes under your center of mass so your upper body never lags behind and you can start a new stride by lifting the leg instead of pushing off, thus

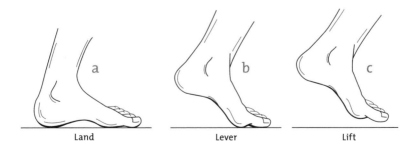

| Land | Lever | Lift |

Figure **4.4** | *Running gait*

making it easier to run with a quick cadence, less impact, less rotational force, and less use of propulsive muscular force.

Are there still times when you might be forced into a heel-striking gait? Yes; depending on what's on your feet. If you're running down a steep hill wearing traditional shoes, you're going to hold your upper body back a bit and strike on your heels to control your speed. Consider how differently you'd handle that hill barefoot or in minimalist shoes that allow natural running form. You would not strike on your heels. Your forefoot would sense the ground initially, thereby regulating your impact and speed and putting your body into a more balanced, agile position.

Sprinting Gait

This gait is all about power. It might seem like an extension of the running gait, but it's really unique unto itself. (See Figure 4.5.) It essentially requires enormous muscular force in short bursts that demand a super-fast stride cadence. Everyone can sprint for short periods of time, but it takes a fine-tuned specimen to be able to sprint fast for 100, 200, or 400 meters. Even for the most elite athletes, it's not possible to sustain that kind of gait and hold form for more than about 500 meters. The body's ability to process oxygen efficiently in a power-induced sprinting gait tends to wane between 300 and 500 meters, depending on the speed and relative fitness of the athlete. Competitors in 800-meter and mile races still run quite fast and at times are in a modified sprinting gait (such as on the last lap), but they're mostly in a running gait until the final sprint.

I have been preaching the differences among the three gait styles for years, and this was one of the factors that led me to launch Newton Running in 2007. So naturally it was no surprise to me and many other running form coaches around the world, such as Malcolm Balk, Danny Dreyer, and Ken Mierke, as well as *Born to Run* author Chris McDougall and others, when a January 2010 study from Harvard researcher and evolutionary biolo-

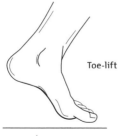

Toe-lift

Figure **4.5** | *Sprinting gait*

gist Daniel Lieberman reported that when running barefoot, humans typically land with a midfoot or forefoot strike that, either barefoot or with shoes on, has less impact on the body than a heel-striking gait. Another study, from the University of Virginia, showed that there are considerably more impacts and shearing forces on the knees, pelvis, and spine while running in shoes with elevated heels than there are when running barefoot (Kerrigan et al. 2009).

Prove this to yourself. Remove your shoes and run across a flat, smooth surface. Your mind and body know what to do. Barefoot, you are not subject to the influence of having your balance altered with gravity by anything under your foot, such as the foam midsole of a running shoe. You have maximized your sensory input from your forefoot for proprioceptive responses to the ground, instead of them being dampened by foam. You will not strike your heel or run way up on your toes; you will land lightly on your midfoot or forefoot, shorten your stride, lean slightly forward with your upper body, and lift your foot off the ground instead of pushing off.

Everyone is a natural runner. Whatever your age, weight, or height, if you run barefoot, you start out balanced with gravity and have your natural ability to sense the ground maximized. You can self-regulate your impact and coordinate whole-body movement to run naturally.

Running and Footwear

So far I have discussed humans moving without the influence of footwear, or running unshod. What happens when you put your current running shoes on? How do your foot strikes and whole body movements change?

The process of sensory communication from your feet is at its best when you are barefoot. That sensory interaction still happens if you're wearing shoes, but it works a heck of a lot better if you can feel the ground through your shoes. If your foot is raised high off the ground, as is the case with many traditional running shoes with foamy midsoles, the sensory input is dampened considerably. Complicating that situation further is that the elevated heel of most running shoes (most shoes are 10–18mm higher in the heel than the forefoot) makes it difficult to land with a natural foot strike at the midfoot section of the foot. The elevated heel gets in the way and is the first part of the shoe to hit the ground. Also, the moment you step into those shoes, your body readjusts its position to compensate for the lifted heel in that shoe.

What does that position look and feel like? (See Figure 4.6.) You can find out right now. While standing on a hard surface, place something small—about the thickness of a small book or deck of cards—under your heels and stand up straight with your arms at your sides. When you do that, notice how your weight shifts back slightly to keep you balanced. Your head moves slightly backward, your lower back arches a little bit, your hips tilt forward, and more weight is applied to your heels, but you are still stable and balanced with gravity.

Once again, starting with the base that your feet provide, your body will find a balanced position with gravity. This happens whether you're wearing thin moccasins or high-heeled cowboy boots or even women's high-heeled dress shoes. Unless your foot is level, your body

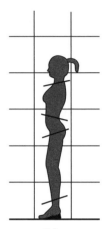

Figure **4.6** | *Elevated heel*

always needs to compensate to achieve balance. When your heels are raised off the ground—as in typical running shoes—you'll put more strain on your lower back and have a need to shift weight backward to maintain that balance. It's not easy, natural, or efficient to run in that position, and it ultimately counters your optimal running form and economy.

5
Foot Biomechanics
A Close Examination

If you spent your entire life barefoot, your feet would look quite a bit different than they do now. They would most likely have very tough skin on the bottom rather than the relatively tender skin that most of us have. They would be wider and flatter, and the muscles and connective tissue inside the feet would be fit and strong.

Natural running form starts with the feet, and to be efficient and smooth when running long distances, you *must* have strong feet and flexible calf muscles. In western culture, the feet do not generally get the kind of strengthening required for safe, strong barefoot running. If your feet have been bound up inside some type of footwear since you were a baby, as is the case for most of us, then they are probably weaker than you realize. The good news is that you can condition your feet to be stronger by walking around barefoot or carefully running barefoot (discussed in more detail in Chapter 9). I often discuss this idea with runners interested in experimenting with running barefoot, reminding them that they should spend no less than a year slowly building the muscles in their feet before running barefoot for longer distances on a regular basis.

Barefoot Around the World

On several occasions I have had the pleasure to run with Zola Budd Pieterse, a native of South Africa who was the last runner to compete barefoot in the Olympics. At her prime as a teenager in the mid-1980s, she set world records on the track in the 2,000m, 3,000m, and 5,000m and won two world cross-country championships while running barefoot.

Zola grew up barefoot and felt most comfortable competing barefoot on the track, although she says she'd often tape her forefeet to protect herself from the abrasion of the track surface. She admitted that training in urban areas on unnatural surfaces could be very hard on the feet and body—too hot, too rough, too much direct impact—which is why she wore shoes while training. We talked about her barefoot running and how strong her feet were back then. As she got older, she ran barefoot less and less and accordingly lost some of that strength in her feet. She felt that training barefoot to strengthen her feet on natural surfaces and retaining that natural running form and sensitivity when running with shoes on unnatural surfaces is a great combination for injury prevention.

One of the primary reasons world-class runners from Kenya, Ethiopia, and other East African countries are such renowned distance runners is that they grew up barefoot and ran and walked barefoot into their late teens or early adulthood. Thus they have strong feet and excellent sensory interaction with the ground surface, which allows them to run with natural, efficient form. In Japan and many other Asian cultures, people go barefoot or wear thin, lightweight slippers inside their homes and use thin sandals and minimal or flatter footwear while outside in order to be more grounded to the earth. Based on that philosophy and the notion that wearing those types of footwear builds strong feet, it's no surprise to see most elite Japanese runners training and racing with a distinctly natural, fluid form.

I have run in South Korea and have come upon exercise areas set aside for the general public. These are open areas in parks or along walking trails that include some general fitness equipment and areas to stretch and perform martial arts. Many incorporate foot exercise areas as

Figure **5.1** │ *Natural running on a natural surface*

well, where stones of various sizes have been cemented to the ground for people to walk across barefoot. Foot reflexology, as it is called, exercises and stimulates pressure points or meridians of the feet with a goal of overall body health. This activity also creates stronger feet and increases the ability to communicate with the ground as well as to self-regulate body pressure on the feet.

Running Surfaces: Natural Versus Unnatural

There is nothing more natural than running barefoot on natural surfaces. When you run on soft grass, sand, or dirt, your body senses that the safest and most efficient way to have your feet land on the ground is with very light forefoot steps (see Figure 5.1). Many of us like the thought of just getting rid of our footwear and running barefoot. It can be done, but as mentioned above, it takes time and patience. Just as with exercising any part of your body, you must build up structure and strength in your feet.

Natural running surfaces, such as a packed sandy beach or a grassy golf course, are ideal to run on because they're soft and predictable, accommodating your unique foot structure and ability to adapt to the surface. In fact, a foot imbalance that manifests when you are running on paved roads or concrete sidewalks may suddenly become a nonissue on natural surfaces. Why is this so?

As you run, landing lightly on your midfoot or forefoot, you sink down into the earth, and in essence the surface comes up to adjust to the imbalance of your feet. The sand, grass, or dirt fills forefoot imbalances you might have, providing a natural forefoot correction. As your foot settles to the ground, the arch and heel get the same filler from the earth. Call it nature's gait-correcting orthotics! The earth conforms to the contours underfoot no matter your foot type. Now that the foot has settled and you have loaded your elastic recoil, you simply lift off, and running seems effortless. This is the way we were all born to run, landing lightly on a natural surface with little impact. You sense the ground with your forefoot and adjust your body posture to work with gravity. Very little energy is wasted between the foot and the ground interface.

Conversely, running with traditional running shoes on unnatural surfaces (such as asphalt or concrete) puts an artificial interface between the foot and the ground. The hard ground surface cannot accommodate individual foot biomechanics in the way a natural surface can, and because our sensory input is dampened by soft shoes, our ability to biomechanically adjust is also greatly limited. Unlike on ever-changing natural surfaces, we have the same rotational movement over and over again for each step of every mile. While making the same repetitive motions on concrete or asphalt, even very small abnormal foot movements can cause wear and tear on muscles, joints, and tendons over time.

A close examination of your own feet will allow you to determine what irregularities you have, if any, and how these could prove to be problematic.

Examining the Foot

Feet play a preeminent role in the whole-body movement for any type of gait. They engage and sense the ground, relay information back to the brain on how to move, and ultimately serve as the primary mechanism for balance. They also allow us to brake, adapt, stabilize, and propel our bodies in all directions. As a runner, your feet just may be the most important part of your body. Yet most runners take their feet for granted, paying little attention to them unless something goes wrong or hurts. That's understandable because so much of what your feet do seemingly involves little or no conscious effort.

Feet are complicated devices, incorporating 26 bones, 100 muscles, and 200,000 nerve endings plus a vast network of ligaments, tendons, fascia, blood vessels, and skin. A close inspection of your feet will reveal subtle differences that have a major impact on the way the rest of your body moves, including your running mechanics. Even if your feet are the same length, they might vary in myriad other ways, including width, flexibility, range of motion, structure, strength, and stability. You're born with some of those differences. Others you acquire through the years based on daily habits; the types of shoes you wear; minor or major injuries; or unknowingly favoring one side over the other because of a twisted pelvis, leg-length imbalance, or muscular imbalance. Even without an obvious debilitating injury, minor changes or differences in your feet—as well as other indicators such as calluses, blisters, bony buildups on joints, or pain in the heel or ball of the foot—can have major impacts on how you run.

Regions of the Foot

The foot is segmented into three regions—the rear foot, midfoot, and forefoot (see Figure 5.2)—and it's important to know the unique role each segment plays in a natural running cycle.

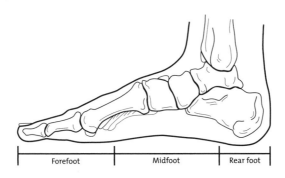

Figure **5.2** | *Three parts of the foot*

The rear foot contains the heel and ankle system and specializes in braking (when in a walking gait) and adapting and balancing. The calcaneous (heel) bone plays a prominent role in balancing the body as the heel settles and allows for elastic recoil, but it was not meant to endure the hard impacts of running.

The midfoot is mainly described as the arch region, which when running with foot strikes near the metatarsal heads acts as a natural suspension system in conjunction with your ankle, legs, and core. When the foot hits the ground, the impact of that contact is immediately controlled, dispersed, and softened through the combined action of numerous muscles and movements in your foot, ankle, lower leg, upper leg, hips, core, and lower back. Striking at the midfoot also puts the ankle in a stabilized or locked position when the upper body mass is directly over the midfoot. Ultimately the muscles, fascia, and bones in the midfoot act as a stabilizer and suspension system between the rear foot and the levering of the forefoot.

Finally, the forefoot encompasses the ball of the foot and the toes. Here we have high sensory input, leverage, and propulsion as we leave the ground.

Foot Types

Beyond these divisions, which all feet share, there are four basic foot types, ranging from a very flat foot to a foot with a very high arch. Knowing which type you have is key to helping you address footwear needs and to better understand how to improve your running mechanics. I provide helpful descriptions and illustrations below, but the best way to determine your foot type is to see a podiatrist or footwear specialist with an under-standing of the foot.

Rigid Flat Foot

Rigid flat feet are flat to the ground and have little to no arch and minimal rotation. This is one of the least common types of foot. Populations that go barefoot tend to have flatter feet, but some folks are naturally born with flat feet. A rigid flat foot can be fairly stable but also difficult to fit into traditional running shoes, which are built with high arch supports, because the foot shape is wider than the typical modern last, which tends to be cut away in the arch.

Flexible Flat Foot

The most common foot type, the flexible flat foot has a relatively high to normal arch height, but an overpronation occurs when walking or running with a heel-striking gait. When landing at the midfoot or forefoot and late-stage pronation occurs, there tends to be moderate to excessive forefoot imbalance. This type of foot tends to toe out or strike more to the lateral edge of the foot to overcompensate for the inward crash. The subsequent inward roll creates excessive rotation to the lower leg, knees, hips, and back.

Neutral Foot

This is a lucky foot type and more rare, with only a small percentage of runners having neutral feet. It is lucky because it typically has few flaws and is the easiest to fit into shoes. It's characterized by a normal arch height and does not have excessive movements in the rear foot or forefoot. A downfall is that when landing with a heel-striking gait, it requires excessive force to push off while starting a new stride, and that can lead to plantar fascia problems, as well as strained propulsive tissue (Achilles tendon and soleus, gastroc, and hamstring muscles). However, when landing on the forefoot the knee tracks over the level forefoot and carries the level position to the hip and lower back. In other words, it does what you want it to do without any drama, which means you can adapt to natural running pretty easily.

Rigid Foot

This type is characterized by a very high arch, with a heel position that tends to be higher than the forefoot. Someone with this foot type can have both supination of the rear foot and, when midfoot/forefoot landing rolls outward, a lateral forefoot imbalance. With a heel-striking gait, this foot type often causes lateral stresses and impact stresses in the ankles, knees, hips, and lower back, as well as iliotibial band strain.

The Wet Test

The sure way of understanding your own foot type is by seeing a podiatrist, but there is a basic test you can do for a clue about what your foot type might be. Called the wet test, it involves imprinting a wet footprint on a piece of paper to determine what kind of arch you have.

Fill a pan or bucket with water and then submerge the bottom of your foot. Remove your foot and quickly step onto a brown grocery sack, newspaper, or dark-colored construction paper. Push your foot straight down and quickly remove it. Look at the shape left by your wet foot to identify the heel, midfoot (or arch), and forefoot and see if it fits one of the images in Figure 5.3.

Flat (or Low) Arch

If you see a big, wide footprint in which the forefoot tapers down gradually to the heel, you probably have a fairly flat (or low) arch (Figure 5.3a). Such a static test might suggest you have a rigid or flexible foot, but you can do a one-legged deep knee bend with upright posture to confirm your self-analysis. If your ankle and midfoot roll inward immediately and dramatically as you begin the squatting motion and your knee starts to track inward, you're overpronating and likely have a fairly flat and flexible foot; the forefoot is adding to the rear foot overpronation. If you're squatting and your ankle and foot are stable and your knee continues to track forward over your lower leg, it's a good sign that you have a rather stable forefoot.

High Arch

You might see the other extreme on the paper with your wet footprint: a fairly smallish space for your forefoot that tapers back sharply to the lateral (outside) of the foot, so much that you might see the heel print as a separate imprint, just a

Foot Imbalances

Many people have imbalances in the length and structure of their metatarsal bones, as well as issues with the stability of the metatarsal joints, all of which affect foot mechanics. These imbalances can cause rotational forces just prior to the foot leaving the ground. This means the ankle will move and pronate as the medial forefoot misalignment gets down to the surface, or the ankle will supinate as the lateral forefoot misalignment gets down to the surface. (Remember that the rear foot is the great adapter round ball that is nearly or completely disconnected from the rest of the footprint (Figure 5.3b). This means you have a high to very high arch and could be an under-pronator or supinator, but you could also be a fairly neutral runner if you have strong, developed feet.

Normal (Medium) Arch

If you see something that's somewhere in between the two prints just described, such as a wide forefoot print that tapers down gradually to the midfoot/arch region (but still leaves a wet spot that's an inch or wider) and then widens back to a round heel imprint, you likely have a medium arch (Figure 5.3c). It's called a normal arch because it typically leads to normal pronation.

Remember, pronation is a naturally occurring function of the foot when you're balanced on your heel or striking at your heel. It doesn't have to be the four-letter word that major shoe companies have made it out to be, especially because it virtually disappears when you land at your midfoot and turn your heel and ankle from a system of loose adaptation to one that is locked out and stable.

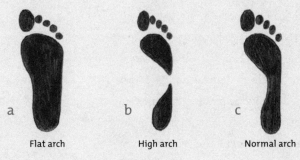

| a | b | c |
| Flat arch | High arch | Normal arch |

Figure **5.3** │ *Results from the wet test*

for all surfaces, even the forefoot imbalance. So when the forefoot is not sitting level with the rear foot, the rear foot will shift in the direction the forefoot moves.)

One such imbalance is called forefoot varus. It can cause late-stage pronation or inward collapse of the foot as it leaves the ground.

Forefoot varus is evident when the ankle is neutral and the forefoot is pitched. The ankle now pronates to get the forefoot on the ground (see

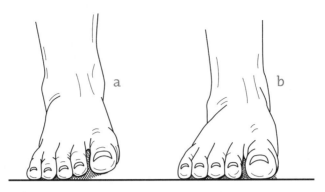

Figure **5.4** | *Forefoot varus without and with correction*

Figures 5.4a and b). The best way to eliminate that imbalance and stabilize your forefoot is by inserting a custom-crafted varus wedge—a firm piece of lightweight beveled foam that levels off the misalignment—under the medial side of the forefoot.

Morton's foot type can also cause late-stage pronation. It is evidenced when the ankle is neutral and the first metatarsal is short and up in the air (see Figure 5.5). The ankle pronates to get the first metatarsal on the ground as the foot moves forward from heel-strike or mid-stance. The simple way to adjust for Morton's foot type is to add a wedge of foam known as a Morton's Extension underneath the first metatarsal joint.

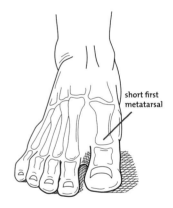

short first metatarsal

Figure **5.5** | *Morton's foot type*

Another forefoot rotational possibility is forefoot valgus, which is evident when the ankle supinates to get the lateral forefoot to the ground (see Figures 5.6a and b). This imbalance is the reverse of forefoot varus. The lateral side of the forefoot is pitched upward, and the ankle supinates to get the imbalance down to the ground. The simple way to adjust for this problem is to add a firm piece of lightweight beveled foam, called a valgus wedge, under the lateral side of the forefoot.

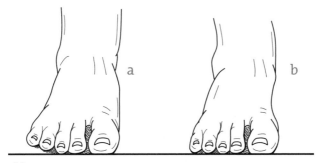

Figure **5.6** │ *Forefoot valgus without and with correction*

Now that you have an understanding of foot types and conditions, let's examine how running with shoes on unnatural surfaces impacts your foot biomechanics.

Overuse Injuries

Different foot types and conditions can lead to a variety of overuse injuries, particularly when paired with a heel-striking gait, an imbalanced forefoot, or other form abnormalities. I address running injuries in Chapter 7, but generally speaking, excessive rotational forces on the foot—either overpronation or oversupination—from a heel-striking gait can lead to overuse injuries throughout your body. If your foot is rotating excessively, your ankle, lower legs, knees, thighs, hips, and lower back are also twisting. That upstream twisting, combined with the heavy impacts of heel striking, leads to a variety of injuries common to runners, including IT band syndrome, shin splints, Achilles tendinitis, plantar fasciitis, patellofemoral pain syndrome, lower back pain, and stress fractures.

These can be frustrating, not to mention painful, situations for anyone, but they are especially so for a runner trying to stay fit or train for a race. If you have experienced any of these ailments, you're not alone. Studies (e.g., Van Mechelen 1994; Van Middelkoop et al. 2008) show that half of all runners are injured every year, and those statistics have been virtually the same for 25 years.

It doesn't have to be that way. There is a better way to run, a more natural way to run, that can reduce or eliminate most of the problems caused by excessive rear foot rotational forces inflicted on the body from running with a heel-striking gait—or in other words, from running with a walking gait.

Avoid Injuries with a Natural Running Gait

Your specific foot type becomes less of an issue when you're running with a natural midfoot/forefoot gait that mimics the properties of a barefoot running style.

As discussed in Chapter 4, recent research from leading universities has shown that we naturally run with light foot strikes at the midfoot/forefoot region of the foot under our center of mass. Running with that kind of natural gait pattern, we simply do not have to worry as much about rear foot biomechanical issues (overpronation and oversupination) as we do when we strike at our heels. By striking at the midfoot, we have completely bypassed the ankle's braking and adapting movement. The foot is stable and locked when the upper body mass aligns over a midfoot foot strike. If you have a neutral or stable forefoot, your foot and body are completely balanced and set up perfectly to leave the ground and start the next stride with minimal rotational forces. If you have an unstable forefoot position, you will have late-stage pronation or supination of the forefoot.

Because rear foot rotation is minimized when the forefoot is stable and level with midfoot/forefoot foot strikes, your upper and lower body will automatically align nicely over the foot. Subsequently, you eliminate excessive propulsive forces because you can lift your leg and foot to start a new stride instead of pushing off. Just like that, you'll be running with natural running form.

Running with Shoes

When running with traditional shoes and a repetitive stride pattern on hard, flat surfaces, such as concrete or asphalt, our feet cannot adjust to the ground—especially when heel striking. Thus, our feet overcompensate while trying to seek out the ground, accentuating the impact and rotational forces of the foot.

If the center of mass is altered by high-heel running shoes and the runner must adjust for the footwear, there will be visible movements revealed in the wear patterns on the outer soles of the shoes. One side of the shoe might be worn down more than the other, for example. But that's only one aspect of what is going on. In fact, something quite different may be happening with the foot inside the shoe. Unfortunately runners and retail shoe salespeople rarely examine the sock liners of their shoes to discover the whole story. For the past 22 years in our lab at Active Imprints in Boulder, Colorado (now the Newton Running Lab), we have used sock liner wear patterns as a way of determining what the foot is doing inside the shoe, rather than focusing on the overcompensation wear seen in the rubber on the bottom of the shoe (as demonstrated in Figures 5.7 and 5.8). This key information from the liner helps us better understand the imbalances

Figure **5.7** | *Outside of shoe shows wear on the lateral side*

Figure **5.8** | *Rubber outsole shows wear on the lateral side*

Figure **5.9** | *Sock liner shows wear on the medial side*

that need correcting in the forefoot to allow for more neutral and efficient foot mechanics.

Asking a few simple questions can get to the root of what's actually happening. For example, a runner might come to me to troubleshoot a problem that he suspects is due to oversupination. I ask what kind of shoes he runs in. Usually it's some kind of stability shoe with a firm wedge of foam acting as a support on the medial (arch) side of the foot. I look at the outsole wear and find that he is striking primarily on the lateral side of the shoe. Then I take the sock liner out of the shoe, which clearly shows wear on the medial side, indicating late-stage overpronation from the heel to toe-off (Figure 5.9); in other words, the *opposite* of what the outsole wear pattern indicates.

The innersole or sock liner shows the true foot movement, and the outsole shows the resulting overcompensation. Without realizing it, this runner strikes the ground to the outside edge of his foot to take more time to adapt to the surface before the foot on the inside of the shoe collapses hard to the inside. This overcompensation increases the time spent rotating, creating additional problems. That outside-to-inside rotation imposes more torque on all the joints and connective tissue in his feet and lower body. Getting a true picture of what is going on helps me solve his real issues.

Generally speaking, several things are happening when you run in modern running shoes with traditionally lifted heels. For starters, as discussed, you have a high heel that gets in the way of the foot landing parallel to the surface. This causes more braking/impact force and rear foot rotational force on the whole body. Time is wasted between initial braking and mid-stance (longer time on the ground, more rotational and impact forces). Now you must push off hard to get started again, creating the vertical oscillation (or bouncing) that leads to highly inefficient running mechanics. As a result you use far more energy to run and endure much more impact from the unnatural surface.

The nature of the material in the forefoot of running shoes is also a factor in forefoot instability. A runner with forefoot varus crashes and rotates the forefoot to try to get to the ground, because the forefoot is not making even contact inside the shoe. As this happens, the runner begins to break down the interior of the shoe foam. She is actually increasing both the amount of time and the magnitude of rotational forces before leaving the ground. Add the hard muscular push-off to get going again, and this movement puts strain on the plantar fascia, Achilles tendon, calf muscles, medial knee, iliotibial band, and hip. The same movements are seen with Morton's foot type.

If someone has forefoot valgus, his feet roll off to the outside of the shoes, and the lateral shifting gets worse as the midsole foam breaks down in that direction. The lateral ankle, knee, hip, and back will overstress from this angle if the forefoot is not supported with a valgus wedge.

Another issue is that runners' feet change over time, and it is common for the metatarsal arch of the forefoot to "drop" (see Figure 5.10). The normal metatarsal area is slightly arched from the sides of the foot and slightly higher in the center. When weighted, the ball of the foot flexes level to the surface it is on. This is the best position in which to sense the ground. When the metatarsals are dropped in the center, pressure is then applied to the center region of a shoe's foam interior and starts to form a hollowed-out space in the foam. The metatarsal heads move up and down against each other instead of being supported by a firm surface. This shearing motion between the interspaces of the met heads, as they are sometimes called, can cause friction on nerves. As the nerves become inflamed and enlarged from the friction, a runner can develop a neuroma, severe pain in the ball of the foot in the inter-spaces of the metatarsal heads. The solution is to support the metatarsal heads in a more natural position with a metatarsal pad. Also, without the forefoot being balanced inside the shoe, the runner sinks into the foam forefoot interior and creates two to three times more rotation than is natural.

By understanding your forefoot biomechanics and balancing accordingly, you can eliminate or highly reduce problematic forefoot misalignments. You can then place your foot parallel to the ground and lift off from

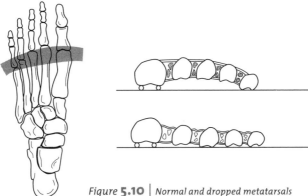

Figure **5.10** | *Normal and dropped metatarsals*

a neutral position. The forefoot, ankle, knee, and hip will align more vertically and be more protected from the repetition of rotational forces when running on hard, unnatural running surfaces.

Runners of all types and abilities can benefit from correcting forefoot imbalances. I help correct forefoot imbalances all the time, from recreational runners stopping in at the Newton Running Lab to world-class athletes such as Ironman world champion Craig Alexander, who, with a Morton's Extension under his first metatarsal, is able to run from a forefoot balanced position and be one of the fastest and most efficient runners in the world of triathlon.

I cover more about foot mechanics as they relate to optimal running form in Chapters 6, 7, and 8. For now, it's important to remember how all the aforementioned foot properties combine to allow for natural running form on unnatural surfaces.

6

The Physics of Running
Whole-Body Kinematics

Natural running is a whole-body movement. Previous chapters focused on foot types, foot discrepancies, and gaits. However, it's important to understand that natural running is not just about where or even how the foot strikes the ground. It is a *whole-body movement* that is coordinated by an instinctive mind–body connection. The many motions your body makes when running are choreographed and orchestrated by the brain as it continually tries to rebalance your body with gravity.

As discussed in Chapter 4, with any movement we make, athletic or otherwise, our brains gather information through our nervous system and use it to put our bodies in the proper position to continue that movement or prepare for any anticipated change. For example, if you walk up a flight of stairs, your brain senses that there is a hard surface beneath and that each stride requires a significant upward lift in which your foot must, for example, go up 12 inches and forward 12 inches before touching the ground and starting the process of becoming balanced again. Your brain immediately understands that spatial exactness as well as the rhythm necessary and puts your body through an intricate set of movements that allow you to climb those stairs.

Another example is jumping rope, which is a simple activity but requires a different level of attention, proprioception, cadence, and balance. You have to twirl the rope over your head and then hop over the rope with such a cadence that it all becomes one fluid motion. Like walking stairs or running, jumping rope requires whole-body kinematics.

First, it's important to note that when you leap off the ground, you do so from the athletic position discussed in the Introduction, using flexed knees and ankles as your natural suspension system for just about any athletic move you make. Second, when you leap up, you land lightly on your forefoot. As you make each leap, your body and arms are positioned so that you are able to land in a balanced position while continuing the momentum and cadence of both jumping and twirling the rope.

This same need for whole-body kinematics applies to other dynamic movements, including running and any uniquely random motions. If you were to put your body in an awkward position, such as dangling atop a chain-link fence, and then hop to the ground, your body would try to put you in position to land as safely and softly as possible. On the first try, you might crash awkwardly to the ground. But if you were to do it several times in a row, your body would fine-tune its adjustments based on what it knows of the height of the fall and the details of the ground. After multiple times doing the same thing, you would land as lightly and efficiently as possible, because the brain would have gained an understanding of the height you're dropping from, the surface you're on, and how to land safely and become centered with gravity.

There is a direct correlation between a random act like that and how your body reacts to running barefoot as opposed to in highly cushioned running shoes. Your brain determines the most efficient, effective, and safest way to run. If you are wearing a traditional running shoe, your brain allows a heel-striking gait because that is perceived to be the most efficient way to run given the shoes' cumbersome geometry. Although this is clearly not the optimal way to run, your brain is choosing what is practical in the moment rather than anticipating the long-term negative effects. However, if you're barefoot, it will have you run with a midfoot/forefoot gait and land lightly on the ground. Don't confuse adaptation with natural movement. Modern runners have *adapted* to traditional running shoes, becoming efficient at running inefficiently.

Maximizing the Mind–Body Connection

When running naturally, two major factors allow us to snap into the best, healthiest, and most efficient running posture. The first is being neutral or balanced with gravity. The second is sensory input derived from your feet, specifically the forefoot. The brain is such a proficient computer that when all the data are streaming properly, it can almost instantaneously respond to what you want your body to do while running. If you're running with good natural running form, you don't need to think about how your head, arms, and torso should move because the mind–body connection takes care of it.

As mentioned previously, gait analysis patterns and several scientific studies have shown that when running naturally or barefooted, humans will touch the earth with a midfoot or forefoot landing. When running naturally, your forefoot senses the ground the instant it touches down, starting the kinematic chain that determines your running mechanics and puts you in the most efficient and effective position for the terrain you're on. Unconsciously, you alter your form slightly on different types of terrain and in different conditions—slippery, wet, dry, rocky, muddy, steep, flat—because your brain takes the sensory feedback from the forefoot's interaction with the ground and positions your body accordingly.

This ability can be compromised if your body is trying to overcome other variables: a physical deficiency you were born with, a past injury, a bad habit, an imbalanced position caused by your shoes, or a lack of feedback between your foot and the ground. Still, your brain helps the body make adjustments to find the proper balance with gravity based on the compromises it has to make. Those adjustments affect the whole-body kinematics for any dynamic movement.

The Impact of Shoes on Kinematics

Some of the variables that compromise our ability to run naturally are beyond our control. They can be overcome, but it's a long process. Shoes, on the other hand, are a choice we make every day, and this choice can negatively impact our posture and create bad habits. This is true of both running shoes and the shoes we wear for work or play.

Because the body needs to always be in balance with gravity, anything that is put under the foot to put it out of a level, balanced position will cause the whole body to react and try to center itself. In other words, the whole body compensates for imbalanced footwear, whether it's a high-heeled dress shoe, dusty old cowboy boot, 1980s-era moon boot, or popular running shoe.

If you wear shoes with a steep ramp angle created by a heel lifted 12–15mm higher than the forefoot (as is the case in most running shoes of the past 30 years), your body will try to overcome that tilted position to become balanced. Even if you are standing still, your body seeks balance. Your knees become locked instead of being the pliable spring suspension systems they're supposed to be. Your hips tilt forward, your lower back arches, and your upper torso tips backward. More pressure is put on your knees, hips, and lower spine.

This is hardly an optimal position. If you try to run in such a position, your body must continue to compensate. With each step, it tries to return to that compromised balanced-with-gravity standing position. The most common result is a heel-striking gait; the braking motion involved with heel striking allows your body to quickly get balanced. That's why some runners insist, "I'm a natural heel striker" or "I heel strike when I get lazy." The truth is, this has nothing to do with being natural or lazy and everything to do with your brain compensating for the compromised starting position in shoes with a built-up heel.

Let's look at the physics of various body positions based on how the foot interacts with the ground (see Figure 6.1). You can simulate each of these situations by standing barefoot and alternately sliding something with the same thickness as a deck of cards under your heels and then under your toes.

Level Foot

If your foot is level to the ground and your upper body is directly over the foot (as it is when unshod or in a shoe with a level profile), you sense that the balance point is in the midfoot, and thus that is where you will land. You are balanced with gravity in that position, and your brain will position your body with whole-body kinematics similar to those in effect when running barefoot, thus enabling you to run easily and efficiently with natural form.

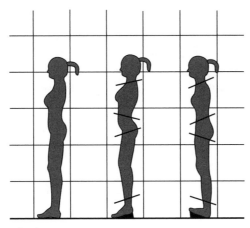

Figure **6.1** | Foot level, elevated on the toe, and elevated on the heel

Elevated Heel

If you elevate the heel by one-half inch to an inch, what happens? You adjust to recenter over the highest point or balance point under your foot. Your hips tilt forward, your lower back arches, and your upper body leans back. Running and trying to land parallel to the ground in this position is a challenge. You will likely run with a heel-striking gait because the robust heel gets in the way and will touch first, or you will feel compelled to touch the heel first because that's where the brain remembers the balancing point to be.

Elevated Toe

What happens if you place the highest point of the shoes under your toes? It's uncommon to see shoes with that kind of geometry, except ballet shoes and basketball training shoes, which are designed to improve jumping power and rebounding skill. In those types of shoes, the athlete will again

Figure **6.2** | *Athlete practicing natural running form*

balance the body over the high point, which is now the toes. The pelvis tips backward, the lower back pushes backward, and the upper body leans forward, plus the calf muscles and Achilles tendon are stretched to maximal positions.

If your starting position is balanced with gravity and your feet are flat on the ground, your body doesn't have to compromise at all. With a slight forward lean, you will start to fall forward. Lift your leg and place your foot level back under your body. Keep repeating this lean and lift—and you are running naturally! (See Figure 6.2.) If you have the chance, observe how young children or most elite-level marathoners run. This is the form you'd see. It's what your body knows from the time you're born and is the most efficient form of running. It allows your muscles, heart, and lungs to exert the least amount of effort while running at any given pace.

Braking, Pushing, and Bouncing

If you have ever run on ice, snow, or any other very slippery surface, you know how critical it is to have your body mass centered over your landing foot. Let's say I am running over ice and I place my heel out in front of my body mass to heel strike. My upper body mass is behind my heel-strike (braking); I slip backward and bust my butt. Conversely, let's say I am running on my toes or pushing off hard (using too much power); I slip forward and fall on my face.

But if I keep my ankles and knees flexed, land lightly on the midfoot/forefoot with my upper body mass directly over my landing, and then simply lift, I have a much better shot at moving safely across the ice. Because I stay centered over my mass, I land lightly, and I lift instead of braking or pushing. This shows how inefficient braking and pushing really are.

As a running form coach, I have been saying for years, "When you are running, friction is your enemy!" Friction is braking, and braking forces slow you down. When you heel strike, there is friction; you see wear on the rubber where you strike the ground. Heel striking also increases the impact and prolonged rear foot rotational forces to the whole body. You now roll forward, pushing off hard or pulling back with the toes (both of which create friction); you overuse power from propulsive muscles and put stress on connective tissue as if you were sprinting.

A little more rare but not uncommon is pointing your toes downward and landing in front of your body on the forefoot and toes. Now the upper body has to take time to get centered over the landing foot, then apply a large propulsive force to take off after what is essentially an act of braking with the forefoot.

Some runners shuffle and scuff the ground with every step, creating noise and friction. That's another form of braking.

To reduce friction while running, you need to sense the ground, land lightly under your center, and lift your feet. By landing under your body mass (center of gravity), you self-regulate your impact by using the lower body to act like a spring, and then you simply lift off the ground with your hip flexors. With the slight lean forward (see Figure 6.3), you move

Figure **6.3** | *Champion triathlete Craig Alexander displays the lean and lift movement.*

up and down less, and thus you endure less impact as well as a forward-vectored return of your own energy.

During my interactions with the advanced engineering class at the Massachusetts Institute of Technology (see Chapter 2), I had the chance to pick the brain of mechanical engineering professor Alex Slocum, who recently started running again. He observed that the running shoe industry is more driven by fancy marketing and sports icon endorsements than by the physics of motion that happens while we're running. He says that the more you look at running with proven science—and specifically the physics of running—the more it makes sense to the runner to optimize body position.

He pointed out that the continual act of braking by striking the ground in front of the body mass, with the upper body leaning backward, greatly counteracts the primary intention of forward motion. Furthermore, applying power to push off hard to keep momentum increases the up-and-down movement called vertical oscillation. In common terms, vertical oscillation is a bouncing effect in which a runner elevates and descends on every stride. The greater the range of vertical oscillation, or the more bouncing a runner does, the less efficient that runner will be. In a natural running gait, vertical oscillation is minimized because there is very minimal braking and no additional required force to push off the ground when starting a new stride (see Figure 6.4).

Figure **6.4** | *Vertical oscillation is minimized when running naturally.*

But with a heel-striking gait, especially one in which a runner has a relatively slow cadence and greater overstrides, the range of vertical oscillation is greatly exaggerated, thus wasting more time and precious energy trying to continue momentum and ultimately making that runner more inefficient.

No matter how high you lift off the ground, gravity always forces you back down. The farther you fall back to the ground, the greater the impact will be when you get there. Slocum points out, however, that gravity doesn't work for or against us when we run. We're working against ourselves if we're running with an unnatural and inefficient heel-striking gait.

Unnatural surface impact forces and power output combined with vibrational forces result in a higher degree of breakdown in the muscle fiber. Thus it also takes more time for muscles to recover from the run.

Running in this fashion also means more time spent getting out of the adapting phase as the foot rotates to get to the ground in order to balance the body, and thus more rotational forces from the rear foot affect the knee, hip, and lower back.

A University of Virginia study headed by Dr. Casey Kerrigan released in December 2009 concluded that there is considerably more impact to the hip, knee, and ankle joints of runners wearing traditional running shoes with elevated heels than to those running barefoot (Kerrigan et al. 2009). The study found an average 54 percent increase in the hip internal rotation torque, a 36 percent increase in knee flexion torque, and a 38 percent increase in knee varus torque when running shod compared to running barefoot. Those additional pressures, the study concluded, can lead to hip and knee injuries and osteoarthritis.

Some coaches will say, "Get a forward pull from gravity." But the "forward pull" from gravity does not work in the strict sense of propelling you forward; your center of mass on average stays the same distance from the ground while running with a natural midfoot/forefoot gait. What the forward upper body position does give you is the ability to run with your foot striking the ground essentially beneath the center of gravity; hence you bob up and down less. The less your center of gravity moves up and down, the more efficient your running will be. This also means the impact forces will be less, so you will have less damage to muscles and joints while running on unnaturally hard surfaces.

As Alex Slocum says, positioning your body so the foot strikes the ground to minimize the up and down motion of the center of gravity is a function of the mechanics of motion of our bodies. Nature evolved us to be efficient running machines, and we evolved barefoot. Runners should recognize how to run barefoot and then get a shoe that allows them to mimic natural running. If you have shoes that allow for landing under the body mass and that lose less energy on impact, you will run more efficiently and with less vertical oscillation.

Running Efficiently and Economically

For years I have read articles about how to become a better endurance athlete through the understanding of science and personal body chemistry. Most of the articles have suggested that you must know two things: your VO_2max (the maximum capacity of the body to transport and use oxygen) and your lactate threshold.

Knowing your VO_2max and your corresponding heart rate training zones allows you to properly train at different intensities. Although your VO_2max drops as you age, that change is so gradual during a particular training season that it's virtually nonexistent. Properly training within those various zones is key to improving your capability as a distance runner.

Knowing your lactate threshold (or aerobic threshold), which is the point at which lactate removal fails to keep up with the rate of lactate production, will give you an understanding of your fitness at a given moment in time. At your personal lactate threshold, there is a sharp increase in blood lactate accumulation and a subsequent fatigue that prevents you from continuing at that level of intensity (or pace). Your lactate threshold is a specific percentage of your VO_2max and can be improved by proper training.

Proper Mechanics

But what about improving running mechanics as a means to improve your efficiency as a distance runner? Discussions of these two factors have been commonplace in articles and training plans for years, but almost inevitably they have suggested that runners who had been running for longer and trained with higher mileage weeks at quicker paces seemed to have better individual running economies.

In this enlightened age, we now know that optimal running mechanics plays a big role in improving running economy, allowing you to run at higher levels of intensity for longer periods of time. (Ultimately, that means you can run a faster 5K, 10K, half-marathon, or marathon.) Alex Slocum explained the principle factor behind it: By running with natural form, your feet land lightly under your center of mass and you bob up and down less.

The bottom line is that running with natural form improves your running efficiency, and unlike with your VO_2max (which is constant) and your lactate threshold (which can be improved over the course of several weeks by proper training), you can start today to make changes to improve your form. This means having your entire body positioned properly so that your heart, lungs, and muscles can exert the least amount of effort for any given speed. The physics of natural running—landing lightly with your midfoot/forefoot under your center of mass, having an upright but slightly forward-leaning posture, swinging your arms close to the body with a 90-degree bend at the elbows, and running with a relatively high cadence—allow for that maximal running economy.

Running economy is important because it is the ultimate factor in deciding how fast you run for your relative fitness and how quickly you recover. For example, if two different people of similar physical makeup and training run for 10 minutes around a track, the runner with the better running economy—the more efficient runner—will run farther than the runner with less efficiency. That's often what makes the difference in an Olympic 1500m race or the New York City Marathon. It's also the ultimate reason any runner should try to transition to a more natural style of running.

As another example, if a runner has been properly training to run a marathon in under 3 hours, the ultimate tool in completing that 26.2-mile race is to make sure she will be able to run with maximal running economy created by the combination of proper training—including having a large aerobic base and fine-tuned anaerobic conditioning—with proper rest, recovery, and tapering time, as well as proper fueling and hydration and optimally efficient running form. If one of those aspects isn't up to par, it will be reflected in her finishing time.

There's no exact science or training chart that can determine which factor is most important. The bottom line is that they're all important, although running economy often gets the least attention. If you're as fit as can be and fully rested when you get to the starting line, but you run with horribly inefficient form, you're going to run slower than you could.

Another MIT class I was involved with set out to quantify how efficient form impacts running economy. I met Steve Lyons at a Multisports.com camp, where he told me he had signed up specifically to change his running form as a means of improving his efficiency and performance. He invited me to be a guest instructor for the MIT chemistry of sport class he and Dr. Patti Christie were conducting on the subject later that fall.

Under the guidance of Christie and Lyons, 25 athletic individuals with various running abilities were put through an eight-week distance-running program that included form clinics on how to run with natural, efficient form. The research was based on them running 4 × 800m or 4 × 1600m repeats while holding a constant heart rate.

The first set of intervals was done in the traditional EVA foam-midsole running shoes that participants started the program with, whereas the latter was done in Newton training shoes. The data revealed that 100 percent of the runners who completed every workout recorded faster times in the final interval wearing Newton shoes. Results showed that 77 percent of the runners ran faster on two or more intervals wearing Newtons, and 55 percent were faster on every interval. A second class with similar results concluded that running with efficient form in shoes designed for a natural midfoot/forefoot gait improved performance. "The results were statistically significant," Christie says. "If you combine the [midfoot] running with the Newton shoes, there was definitely a significant difference" (Christie 2009/2010).

Footwear Affects Form

I had known for years that different types of shoes, combined with improved running mechanics, could play a role in improving running economy. In fact, this was one of the reasons I started Newton Running. In the late 1990s I approached the late Dr. Amy Roberts, a meticulous research scientist and exercise physiologist at the Boulder Heart Institute, about conducting a study that involved five running subjects to determine running economy in their favorite running shoes and in our hand-built prototypes.

She conducted the study and was surprised to see that footwear made a significant difference in the running economy of each of the five subjects. She was also a runner and ran in Newton's early prototypes, discovering that the shoes helped her carry proper running form more easily. After the initial testing she wrote, "This technology demonstrates improved running efficiency in a laboratory setting. Therefore, it is expected that overall performance in the field should also be improved" (Roberts n.d.).

After Roberts moved on to the Boulder Center for Sports Medicine, she continued to work on human performance testing, and we continued our studies as our prototype shoes evolved. She published many papers on exercise physiology and altitude training and tested many local runners and professional athletic teams to set baselines for the individual training programs.

Hardly a day goes by that I do not mention Dr. Roberts's work to someone. We had many discussions about biomechanics and whole-body movement and how the feet function both shod and unshod. She helped me to understand more about natural running form and the influence of footwear on the foot as it relates to cardiovascular performance. She also produced scientific evidence to support what we were doing and saying about running form and shoe design.

Dr. Roberts outlined the biomechanical disadvantages of running in shoes with steep ramp angles:

Decreased Running Performance in Traditional Shoes

- Traditional running shoes have stiff outsoles and thick midsoles that restrict the foot's natural movement. When the foot bends the shoe to move forward, energy is used and lost.
- When running in a traditional shoe, the foot sinks into the shoe's cushion medium. The materials deform under the foot and dissipate energy laterally. This energy cannot be returned to the runner.

Less Efficient Energy Return When Heel-Striking

- When the heel strikes first, the foot is in a braking position and more impact and rotational forces occur.
- When the foot does not land parallel to the ground, the whole body is unbalanced and unable to react quickly; therefore, more energy is lost between the foot and the ground.
- When heel-striking or overstriding (landing in front of the body mass), the foot stays on the ground for a longer period of time (heel-to-toe running). This creates a slower stride turnover rate, or slower cadence, than what is seen in natural running.
- Traditional running shoe materials dampen the forefoot's ability to sense the ground surface and to self-adjust the impact using the whole-body position.

High Running-Related Injury Frequency

- When running in lifted heel shoes and soft midsole materials, the runner heel-strikes as the heel gets in the way of landing parallel to the ground and thus lands with greater impact. The impact leads to increased risk of shin splints, plantar fasciitis, and other related injuries.

After studying the difference in kinematics between barefoot and shod running, Roberts concluded that barefoot running can be seen as the "optimal" biomechanical running condition from which to model a running shoe.

Get Off Your Heels

For years many running form coaches (including myself) have recognized that runners have taken on an unnatural running form. We have gone to great lengths to try to coach runners away from heel-striking and toward landing more under the body. This is the only way to achieve the whole-body kinematics of a natural running gait, because it's the only way to ensure the body is naturally centered with gravity.

Debates abound over how many runners are actually natural midfoot/forefoot strikers. Critics claim that most runners are actually heel-strikers;

indeed, several studies that have observed runners running on unnatural surfaces have proclaimed that 60 to 80 percent of runners heel strike most of the time (Hasegawa, et al., 2007). Those figures might be true, but none of those studies has taken into consideration that the majority of subjects were wearing shoes with an elevated heel and that the high heel generally gets in the way of midfoot/forefoot foot strikes.

Try it for yourself. If you put on a pair of traditional training shoes with a thick foam midsole and a slope angle of 8 to 17 percent (based on a 12–25mm heel/toe differential), you'll find it difficult and not very efficient to run with natural form. Your entire body is in a compromised position while trying to stay centered with gravity in a raised-heel posture. In addition, as your trailing leg swings through the gait pattern, the elevated heel of the shoe tends to scuff, and more likely crash hard into, the ground.

In running laboratories researchers note the difference between barefoot runners and those wearing the modern, supportive, high-end running shoes that are most commonly used by the running public. Their research finds that the shoes impose unnatural angles on the foot, knee, hip, and lower back not seen when running barefoot. It is commonplace in running magazines to see articles on treating common running injuries. In fact, it was because I was seeing and hearing about so many runners with injuries in the 1980s that Jennifer and I started Active Imprints to try to balance people's feet and influence their running form to stave off these chronic running injuries.

Yet up until recently, natural running and barefoot running have been discredited by big running shoe brands, running magazines, and much of the running public because of what might be best called "the more is better syndrome." Fifty years ago, bigger, better, faster was always desirable. In the age of going green, people are realizing that spending more and having more are not the only answers. Wearing overbuilt shoes because "they" say we should is no longer the solution. Those of us in the natural running movement have long known that landing on the midfoot/forefoot protects your body more than a high heel lift running shoe.

Another analogy is the recent rise in popularity of organic and natural foods. When agricultural production became technologically mechanized and the demand for faster production increased, farmers began spraying pesticides on their crops to keep bugs and strains of disease at bay as a means of maximizing their harvest yield and speeding up the seed-to-harvest cycle. The intention was good, but even though the larger fruits and vegetables that grew faster looked great, the nutrients and flavor were often compromised.

The situation is similar with running shoes. The intention of trying to protect runners from the harsh impacts of the unnatural surfaces of concrete and asphalt was good. But elevating the heel of shoes altered a runner's center of mass and severely dampened the sensory input coming from the forefoot. So for years runners have had their running gait negatively altered by footwear that was designed to help.

Based on both professional expertise and his own experience as a runner, Alex Slocum suggests that instead of using artificial means (and overbuilt running shoes) to become a better runner, it makes sense to focus on running with good biomechanics and the whole-body kinematics that are conducive to the physics of natural running. To do so, you need footwear that coincides with midfoot/forefoot foot strikes under your center of mass, not shoes with elevated heels that promote heel striking.

This is not just an academic discussion. Running with inefficient, heel-striking form is at the root of most common overuse injuries. We will examine these injuries in the next chapter, taking a closer look at the reasons they occur.

7
A New Way to Look at Common Running Injuries

In the summer of 1993, Paula Newby-Fraser was suffering from lateral ankle pain that she just couldn't shake. Already a five-time Ironman triathlon world champion, she was only a few months out from defending her most recent title in Kona when she came to my footwear lab in Boulder with what she was afraid might be a career-ending injury.

At that time, Paula could only manage about five minutes of running at a time. She didn't have any pain while riding her bike or swimming (no surprise there, as those are nonimpact, non-weight-bearing activities), and thus she remained very fit from those two sports. However, she knew she had to listen to her body and back off from running until she could solve whatever problem was causing her pain.

I knew she was an efficient, natural runner who ran on her midfoot/ forefoot, and I figured that a forefoot imbalance was most likely causing her ankle problem. My goal was to find the imbalance and get Paula centered with gravity to reduce the negative rotational forces affecting her ankle and maximize her energy output so she could get back to her winning ways.

A word about balance: It is imperative. Virtually every sport requires an athlete to have a balanced forefoot—running, skiing, cycling, tennis, golf. A balanced forefoot is the key to functional and efficient movement through the rest of your body, starting with your foot and ankle and on up through the knees, hips, and upper body. A balanced forefoot gives your body the platform to move through the sagittal, or forward, plane with symmetrical movements.

So I set out to get Paula back in balance. When I looked at Paula's feet, I quickly spotted that the first metatarsal of her right foot wasn't lying flat on the ground. Her feet faced out, or "toed out." When I explained to her about the abduction of her feet, she was quick to tell me she had spent many years as a ballet dancer as a child. I told her that her toed-out position, along with a forefoot rotation from the forefoot imbalance, was crushing the outside of her ankle while running. When the forefoot was stabilized in her cycling shoes, she had more power output.

Athletes like Paula Newby-Fraser work at a high level and typically have a heavy volume of training and racing, so it's imperative that they be über-efficient. Even if the forefoot is out of balance by only a few millimeters, the repetitive rotational forces on unnatural surfaces, or even while pushing down while pedaling a bike, over time and distance can lead to a nagging injury.

I had built custom foot supports for top triathletes Scott Molina, Mark Allen, Mike Pigg, Wolfgang Dietrich, and Paul Huddle; duathlon world champion Kenny Souza; Olympic gold-medal cyclist Alexi Grewal; and Team 7/11 teammate Bob Roll. The word got around Boulder that greater comfort and performance and less wear and tear on the body could be achieved through lightweight foot supports that balance the forefoot.

I told Paula I thought she needed a lightweight foot support with about 3mm of support under her first metatarsal. "Is that it?" she asked. It seemed too simple. "You didn't even look at my ankle." Actually, I had. When she was standing in front of me, I had asked her to bend her knee and ankle forward. I saw her right ankle pronate to get her first metatarsal down to the ground. When I applied a small piece of rigid foam material under the joint and she flexed forward, her ankle stayed in place and didn't pronate. Without the foam support wedge, her ankle was compensating for her forefoot position and causing the injury.

Paula had only seven weeks to get optimally fit before defending her Ironman world championship. After the first week with the new foot support, she was up to 30-minute runs with no pain in the ankle. She kept training hard on the bike and swim, and two weeks before the race, she was up to 90 minutes of running with no pain. Still, she'd have to double that time and add a few minutes if she wanted to run a 3:05–3:10 marathon leg and have the chance of winning another Ironman.

Figure 7.1 | *Paula Newby-Fraser winning the 1994 Ironman triathlon in Kona, Hawaii*

With the high levels of aerobic fitness she had achieved training for the swim and bike, she was the first woman off the bike in Hawaii and started the run with a 10-minute lead. She later admitted that it took a supreme effort to keep moving after the 17-mile mark of the run because the injury had taken a bite out of her run training. But she didn't have any ankle pain, so she was able to muster the strength to hold on. She would go on to win three more Ironman world championship titles (giving her eight overall) and finish her career with 24 Ironman victories. (See Figure 7.1.)

Listen to Your Body

I've been working with injured runners and other athletes for more than 22 years and have been a guest lecturer and hands-on running coach since 1993. I tell this story about Paula before every talk I give to pay tribute not only to her tenacity, but also to her ability to listen to her body. Taking the time to rest and figure out what was wrong was the smartest thing Paula could have done. Had she tried to force the issue and run through the pain, she would have started overcompensating and altered her gait considerably. That could have been a road leading to disaster, because it would have thrown her entire body out of alignment and affected her performance in other sports.

Listening to your body is key to understanding an injury and the first step on the path to getting healthy and staying that way. It's about using common sense and good judgment and being smart about your personal fitness and goals. Listening to your body is a basic instinct that should never be ignored.

In my clinics, I call it the Forrest Gump Rule. If you're tired, rest. If you're hungry, eat. If you're thirsty, drink; your body is telling you you're dehydrated. If you crave chips or pretzels after a workout, eat some; your body probably needs salt. If you're craving a steak or burger, it's probably because you need protein. And as Forrest Gump says, if you gotta go, you gotta go!

Listening to your body can help you manage fatigue, assess your nutritional and hydration needs, and reduce the impact of what could become a debilitating problem. It's your early warning system, alerting you to an oncoming cold or flu or to a developing injury. If you listen closely, you can also assess whether you have done things properly, if you're strong and healthy and ready to push yourself to a solid race effort. Legendary running coach Sir Arthur Lydiard says: "Your biggest gains in training and performance are when you rest the body" (lydiardfoundation.org).

Runners sometimes have a difficult time listening to these signals. What would you do if you were training for a marathon and twisted your ankle a month before the race? Say you rested it, but it didn't seem to be getting better even after several days off from running. Would you go ahead and do the longest run of your 16-week training plan tomorrow, or would you take more recovery time and risk being ill-prepared for your race? Would you rest, or would you push ahead knowing your body could probably handle the minor pain for two and a half hours of running?

The truth is, most of us would ignore the swelling and apply ice, grimace, and suck up the pain, because as athletes, we train ourselves to be tough and tenacious, not wimpy and soft. No pain, no gain, right? Wrong. If you do your long run under those conditions, you'll likely overcompensate and wind up hurting another part of your body. Then you'll have to hobble to the starting line with all of your excuses lined up in your head and probably end up with disappointing results. That's not running, that's a suffer-fest. As Clint Eastwood says in his 1973 Dirty Harry classic *Magnum Force*: "A man's got to know his limitations." The right thing to do is listen to your body, take time to recover, and if necessary postpone your race plans.

If you've been dealing with chronic discomfort or pain for a few years or even a few months, the best thing to do is stop running and take time off to find out what's ailing you. As runners, we can often have obsessive-compulsive tendencies, making it difficult for us to stop running for a single day, let alone several weeks, even if we know that rest might mean eliminating pain and finding a healthier way to run.

Six Simple Tips for Injury Prevention

Common sense is one of the building blocks of injury prevention and natural running. As a coach and camp lecturer, I outline six simple points, which I consider the keys to staying healthy and recovering as quickly as possible:

1. Understand Your Foot Type and Forefoot Biomechanics

Know the basics about your feet. That means knowing your general foot type (discussed in Chapter 5). If you have an imbalance in your forefoot or your feet are weak, use a flexible foot support with your forefoot correction, such as a varus wedge or a Morton's Extension. If you are unsure, ask your podiatrist, physical therapist, general practitioner, or other primary healthcare provider. Going barefoot or using sandals more often will work the feet, strengthening them. (See Chapter 9 for barefoot running drills.) Make this transition slowly, only a few minutes at a time at first, and work up to more over time. The goal is to strengthen and balance your feet.

2. Understand and Practice Natural Running Form

Put simply, have your feet contact the ground beneath your center of mass. From there, you'll be set up for efficient whole-body kinematics. If your foot strikes are slightly in front of your body mass, you're braking and will need to add power to keep moving forward. This will cause you to push up against gravity, and you'll run with less efficiency. With less efficiency, you will need more recovery time from the impact of the surface. You'll also be spending more time on the ground, running slower speeds, and risking the chance of increased impact and counterproductive rotational forces on the rest of the body. (I discuss the execution of natural running form extensively in the next three chapters.)

3. Maintain Range of Motion to Muscles

You do not have to be a yoga guru or a stretching fanatic, but you do need to stay limber. Some folks are naturally flexible in their muscles and connective tissue (flexible flat foot); some are naturally tight in their muscles and connective tissues (rigid foot type/supinator). Thus the need for flexibility or a minimum range of motion for natural running varies from person to person. Getting massages and working on muscle groups with self-massage tools are great ways to break up adhesions to the muscles and allow them to be healthy and fully functioning so joints can also fully function. Massage also flushes out the postexercise lactic acid buildup that can cause adhesions.

Do not ignore overly tight muscles; they can put tremendous stress on connective tissue, which leads to other problems. For example, if your calf muscle group is so tight that you cannot flex your ankle upward to land parallel to the ground, you will either land too far up on your toes and push off hard in sprinting fashion, straining your calf muscles and Achilles tendon, or you will use the opposite side of the leg muscles, the anterior tibialis, to lift the toes and force the ankle to dorsiflex, causing shin splints.

4. Don't Compensate for Injuries, Pain, or Biomechanics

When runners set their minds on a goal, it sometimes becomes more about the goal than about logic, health, or safety. I have run several 100-miles races, and one year while running the Leadville 100 in Colorado's high country, I had an encounter that, unfortunately, is quite typical of many I've had. I was at the 55-mile mark, somewhere above 12,500 feet, when I spied a runner nearby who was using a long stick as a crutch. When I asked him if he was OK, he just looked at me, gritted his teeth, and said, "I am going to do this thing even if it kills me!" Seeing how he looked, I thought he might soon meet his doom with that kind of attitude. Ultimately he didn't finish and was hurting for quite some time afterward. The bottom line is that a "mind over body" mentality is great to a point, but not at the expense of health and safety.

I've been in Kona several times for the Ironman world championships, and in every race you see people who strain their backs by riding their bikes in a very aero position for 7 or 8 hours. They barely make the cut-off to start the run, and instead of heading to the medical tent, knowing they cannot even stand up straight, they proceed to try to run 26.2 miles bowed over with their eyes looking directly at the ground. A few unrelenting souls make it, but most do not. Although finishing Ironman is important, that's not a healthy or safe way to run.

5. Avoid a Fast-Food Mentality

It seems we all want get to where we are going too quickly. I call it the fast-food mentality. Even when it comes to training, we want it our way, and we want it now. It doesn't help that magazines tell us, "Get off the couch and run a marathon in 12 weeks!" That might work for some, but it is a recipe for disaster for others. The intention to inspire folks to become more fit and lead healthier lifestyles is good, but the goal is too lofty. After all, as the story goes, Phidippides, the first marathoner from ancient Greece, died shortly after his heroic run. A more reasonable ramp-up from sitting on the couch might be to run a 5K in 12 weeks and gradually increase your distances from there. For some, even that goal is too lofty for a starter. The point is that you need to be honest with yourself, listen to your body, and start slowly. Do not increase distance, speed, or intensity too quickly.

Running is the only sport in which it seems acceptable not to get any instruction before getting started. It's assumed that you can buy a pair of shoes and hit the ground running without any sense of what proper form is. But the reality is that inefficient biomechanics, bad form, lack of flexibility, form changes too quickly, and overcompensation, along with too much distance, speed, or intensity, can stop you in your tracks.

A better approach is to be patient, get instruction, and focus on proper form. You'll eventually imprint the proper movements into muscle memory, develop strength and flexibility, and begin building on the fundamentals, getting better over time. Taking the time to learn what proper technique is will help you prevent injuries and improve gradually.

6. Listen to Your Body and Learn from Your Mistakes

Despite our best efforts, most runners suffer an injury from running at some point. When it comes to running, there is no such thing as injury elimination. At the very best, the idea is to minimize the frequency and severity of the problems that cause the injuries. Transitioning to natural running form can help eliminate many of the factors that cause overuse injuries.

Impact, Rotational, and Propulsive Forces

The most common running overuse injuries—plantar fasciitis, Achilles tendinitis, shin splints, and iliotibial band syndrome—result from three primary sources: excessive impact forces from braking with a heel-striking gait, excessive rotational forces from that kind of gait, and the subsequent excessive force necessary to push off the ground to start a new stride with that kind of gait.

A closer look at anatomy will help us understand these movements better. It's important to note that the muscles on the front of your legs are considered braking muscles—including the tibialis anterior (shin) and quadriceps group (thigh)—whereas the muscles on the back of the legs—the gastrocnemius and soleus (calf) and hamstring group (thigh)— are considered propulsive muscles that work in concert with the Achilles tendon and other soft tissue connections between the lower leg and the foot (see Figure 7.2).

Most runners are absorbing too much impact from braking and consequently using too much muscle power to maintain forward momentum. These motions create high impacts, longer strides, and a vertical push that takes more power output from propulsive muscles. It's a highly inefficient process with negative effects across the entire body. When running in this fashion, we are isolating braking muscles on the landing and isolating

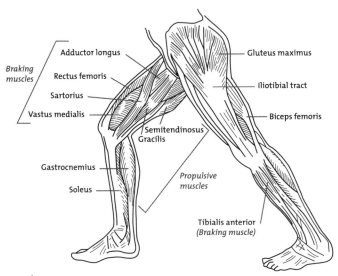

Figure **7.2** | *Leg muscles*

propulsive muscles on the takeoff. That is not how our bodies were designed to run; it's how traditional running shoes have encouraged us to run. We heel strike while running because we *can*, then we push off hard because we *have to* in order to restart momentum and keep up the pace of the run.

When you run with a heel-striking gait, the initial impact with the ground sends shockwaves up your body. Known as impact transients, these shockwaves put enormous strain on your joints, especially the knees, hips, and spine. Not only do these wear away at connective tissue (such as the cartilage in your knees), but studies have shown they can also result in enormous shearing forces in those joints. The leg muscles are also damaged from the impact, which leaves the runner with a longer recovery time and chronically tight muscles (see Figure 7.3).

Running with a natural gait cannot eliminate all running injuries; there are too many factors that can cause problems. But natural running form can reduce or eliminate the primary factors tied to most overuse injuries.

By landing lightly on your midfoot/forefoot and then allowing your heel to settle to the ground before starting a new stride, you're using the muscles, soft tissue, and bones in your foot, ankle, legs, and flexed knees as shock absorbers to greatly reduce the destructive impact transients that

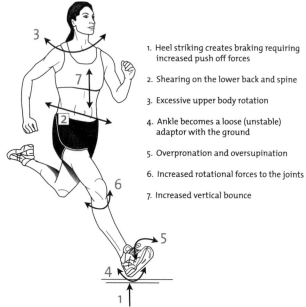

1. Heel striking creates braking requiring increased push off forces

2. Shearing on the lower back and spine

3. Excessive upper body rotation

4. Ankle becomes a loose (unstable) adaptor with the ground

5. Overpronation and oversupination

6. Increased rotational forces to the joints

7. Increased vertical bounce

*Figure **7.3*** | *Heel striking can lead to all kinds of injuries.*

shoot up your body. Running with that type of midfoot/forefoot gait also eliminates most of the rotational forces on your feet, ankles, legs, knees, and hips. Finally, when you use strong core muscles to lift your leg to start a new stride in a natural running gait, you eliminate the excessive propulsive muscular force in your hamstrings and calf muscles.

Common Overuse Injuries

Whether you're a fairly new runner or have been running for years, you've probably had some kind of overuse injury. You're not alone; studies have shown that up to 50 percent of runners are injured every year. Having worked closely with runners for many years, I have seen common groups of injuries and gained an understanding of how they develop and how they can be cured. Some injuries come from impact and rotational forces, others derive from propulsive forces, and some are the result of both.

Following are a few of the most common running overuse injuries and how they occur.

Achilles Tendonitis: Rotational Forces and Propulsive Forces

The Achilles tendon is the large tendon at the back of the ankle that connects the large calf muscles to the heel bone and assists in the elastic recoil process of transferring energy during a running gait. Achilles tendonitis occurs when the Achilles tendon becomes inflamed and tender when it is strained from rear foot or forefoot rotational movements and/or using excessive power to begin a new stride.

Patellofemoral Pain Syndrome: Impact and Rotational Forces

Patellofemoral pain syndrome, or anterior knee pain, is pain at the front of the knee that comes on gradually, with symptoms increasing over a period of time. It occurs when the patella does not move or "track" in a correct fashion when the knee is bent and straightened. This movement can eventually damage the surrounding tissues, such as the cartilage on the underside of the patella itself, which can lead to pain in the region. The primary causes are heavy impacts from a heel-striking gait and the subsequent excessive rotational movement from rear foot or forefoot imbalance.

Iliotibial Band Syndrome: Rotational Forces

The iliotibial band is a sheath of thick, fibrous connective tissue that runs down the outside of the thigh with the purpose of allowing extension of the knee and abduction of the hips. It attaches to a muscle at the top hipbone and runs down the outside of the thigh, connecting with the outside of the shin (tibia) bone. The IT band becomes tight and painful (near the outside of the knee) when a runner strikes the ground at the heel with a fairly straight knee, and then rotational forces that start in the foot force the knee to track inward instead of straight ahead. That pulls the lateral side of the leg and stretches the IT band in the process.

Shin Splints: Impact and Rotational Forces

"Shin splints" covers a variety of types of pain at the front of the lower leg. The most common type is inflammation of the sheath surrounding the tibia bone in the shin, caused by the hard impacts of a heel-striking gait and the excessive rotational forces occurring at the foot and ankle. As the foot and ankle rotate, that twisting motion continues up the body and results in traction forces on the sheath of the shinbone. Overly tight calf muscles are also a cause of shin splints.

Plantar Fasciitis: Impact, Rotational, and Propulsive Forces

Plantar fasciitis is a painful condition caused by overuse of the plantar fascia or the thick arch tendon of the foot. Excessive impact from heel striking, the subsequent excessive rotation of the foot after impact, and the excessive force needed to push off to start a new stride all contribute to the inflammation and straining of the plantar fascia, sapping it of strength and flexibility and ultimately weakening the foot.

Hamstring/Calf/Achilles Strains: Propulsive Forces

Pulling, straining, or tearing a calf or hamstring muscle and straining the Achilles tendon are common injuries in runners that are caused by pushing hard to start a new stride. Those injuries can occur suddenly and unrelated to previous use if, for example, you start charging up a hill without a proper warm-up or are using excessive force early in your run. They can also occur after days or weeks of training in which one or more of the propulsive group (hamstring, calf, Achilles) is fatigued or overworked and forces another to assume more of the propulsive load. For example, if you have really tight or tired hamstrings and cannot lift your leg as you normally might, your calf will put out more effort to maintain your running pace and could become strained as a result. Strains to the propulsive group can also occur as you are trying to transition to natural running, especially if you are making the change too fast or if you are incorrectly pushing off your forefoot (like a sprinter) to start a new stride and not letting your heel settle to the ground.

Knee/Hip/Lower Back: Impact Forces

Numerous types of lower back soreness and strain can occur from running with an inefficient, heel-striking gait. Studies have shown that the excessive impact forces from a heel-striking gait can wreak havoc on the muscles, soft tissue, and joints of the knees, hips, and lower spine. As the impact transients move up the body, they cause an unnatural shearing effect, which can cause acute pain, inflammation, and regional soreness.

Stress Fractures: Impact Forces

Stress fractures are small cracks in the bones of the foot and lower leg, most commonly the metatarsal bones of the forefoot and lower leg (fibula). In some female runners even the femur and hip can receive a stress fracture. Overuse injury stress fractures can be brought on by intensity (too much speed or hills taken too quickly without slow buildup), duration (running too far on long runs without a gradual buildup in mileage), and frequency (doing too many workouts all the time; not enough recovery time). Repetition of hard impacts and running with excessive muscle power to push off the ground overuses the muscles of the lower legs. When the muscles are overworked and fatigued, they are unable to help absorb shock and instead the impact forces are transferred to the bones.

The bottom line is that running with a natural gait in appropriate footwear, mimicking a barefoot running style, is a pathway to healthier and more efficient running.

8

Natural Running, Unnatural World

If I told you there is a way to use less energy and muscle power to run faster and with fewer problems, but that first you would need to understand the principles of the movement, have an open mind, and be patient while your body and mind adjust and relearn how to run naturally, would you do it?

The fact that you bought this book and are reading this right now means your answer is very likely a resounding "yes." Well, there is a better way to run, namely the way your body is naturally inclined to run. The basic idea is that we should run with a barefoot running style, but for a lot of reasons, not necessarily barefoot.

Knowing what you're up against in the modern world as well as something about your own form, basic posture, and foot type, as discussed in previous chapters, is the best place to begin to re-create your form into a more natural one.

Observing literally thousands of runners since 1988, along with helping them overcome some of their running injuries, I have discovered several interesting things about how today's runners operate. Generally speaking, many runners often unknowingly succumb to poor running form over time, influenced by modern running shoes and unnatural surfaces. As runners in a modern world, our form is bound to change if we fail to recognize and adapt to the important and even perilous changes underneath our feet.

We live in a world made mostly of concrete and asphalt; thus we're almost always running on hard, unnatural surfaces. Man-made, unnaturally hard surfaces that we run on were built to drive vehicles on. The term "road racing," often used to describe races from a 5K to a marathon, sounds a lot like cars racing along paved streets. Pavement allows the wheels of a car to roll smoothly and brake efficiently. Although this surface is not ideal for runners, it is the surface on which most modern running races take place, because of the controllable conditions for support and safety of the runners. Most people run most of their miles on hard surfaces most of the time, if only because there is a lack of natural surfaces to run on in population centers.

Another key factor affecting form is footwear. As discussed previously, since the early 1970s the thick, foam midsoles of modern running shoes have been altering a runner's center of gravity and encouraging a heel-striking walking gait while trying to run.

Runners will often say to me, "But I am a natural heel-striker!" I always suggest they take off their shoes and observe their form as they run across concrete. Are they natural heel-strikers then? Definitely not. Their brains won't let them strike at their heels on a hard surface because the enormous impact force would be painful and debilitating.

High-heel geometry and soft midsole material trick us into thinking it is OK or even natural to strike the heel and then push off hard while running. But this is a man-made form of running; it is certainly not how we run naturally.

One way to remedy this is to look for running shoes that are more conducive to natural running biomechanics. Shoes that are lightweight and have a low ramp angle (5 percent or less) encourage a more natural gait in which the foot hits the ground lightly and parallel to the ground—similar to how a bare foot engages the ground.

How light is lightweight? Modern materials and manufacturing techniques, including less stitching, fewer overlays, and lighter midsoles, are allowing shoes to become lighter and lighter. Two or three fewer ounces might not seem like much, but you can feel the difference on your feet once you lace your shoes up, and you'll certainly feel the beneficial effects after a long run. Fewer ounces on every footstep definitely lessen your load over the long haul.

But although lightweight shoes with a near-level geometry are better for all runners, it's not only the weight and design that make the difference. How you use the shoes is also important. In other words, it's about form, specifically natural running form: learning what it is and how to reclaim it.

How We Run: Awkward Deficiencies

Runners come in every shape and size, and so do running styles. As discussed in Chapter 3, many runners have visible form flows, some of which are symptoms or signs of something else happening with their feet. Often the most glaring mechanical deficiencies are the result of compensations the runner is making to try to recenter his body with gravity or continue forward momentum to counteract other energy-wasting movements he might be unknowingly succumbing to. Some of those compensation movements are very common and quite awkward looking, so much so that we can characterize them by what the runner looks like. Following are a few of the more common form compensations I have observed and how to address them.

The Fighter

You can always hear this runner coming up behind you. The Fighter hits the ground with a loud strike of the heel, followed by the foot slapping the ground even louder with double impact. Her upper body is leaning backward, and her shoulders and arms are being torqued across the front of the body. This runner is using way too much power. She looks to be fighting an invisible foe, sort of like a boxing match with gravity. But the winner is, and always will be, gravity.

Quick Fix

Drop your arms to 90 degrees and alternately pull your elbows back when running, then relax and allow your arms to alternately swing forward. The entire motion should be smooth and consistent, but if you have to think about applying energy, think about pushing your elbows straight back and letting the synchronicity of your leg cadence naturally swing them forward. Let yourself fall forward and shorten your stride.

The Shuffler

Like the Fighter, the Shuffler is not using proper whole-body movement to run efficiently. He shuffles the lower legs and does not lift the legs at all. This type of runner thinks he is running efficiently, and at least he does have less vertical bounce than the Fighter. However, he is confined to how quickly he can shuffle the lower legs, and usually the upper body is twisting hard to assist the limited range of motion going on down below. Furthermore, the runner is not utilizing the elastic spring in his legs. And by not putting some power and movement into the running stride, he gets nothing back. It's definitely not efficient.

Quick Fix

Lift the knee a little higher than normal to start each stride, and use a greater hip and leg extension with each stride. (High knee drills, described in Chapter 9, will help to eliminate this form flaw.)

No Arms

Perhaps someone told this runner to conserve energy by letting her arms dangle at her sides or carrying her arms very low and barely moving them. This is utterly inefficient and ineffective. A runner is not saving energy by doing this; rather, she is restricting whole-body coordination, which is essential for efficient running form. Plus, this runner is restricting her cadence, or the frequency of footsteps.

Quick Fix

First, bend your elbows to about 90 degrees, thus allowing your hands and forearms to elevate and create a compact arm swing, then increase your stride cadence. You need this coordinated contralateral movement of your arms and legs alternating in unison to achieve the proper balance and cadence of a running gait.

Chicken Wings

A runner with this form looks like the name sounds. He carries his arms in a high, shrugging position, with his elbows up and away from his body, and overrotates his upper torso as a means to aid forward propulsion.

Quick Fix

Drop your arms to 90 degrees and bring them closer to your body and then alternately pull your elbows back when running. Relax and allow your arms to alternately swing forward. Again, you need the coordinated contralateral movement of your arms and legs alternating in unison to achieve the proper balance and cadence of a running gait.

Running with unnatural running mechanics creates problems, takes too much power, and creates muscle strain. Many runners are actually beating themselves up with bad form. You are simply working against yourself when you're not running with natural form.

Fixing Your Running Form

Be warned: Often when retraining runners to run with more natural running form, I will hear them say that it is harder than the way they currently run. True! I say they have become *efficient at running inefficiently.* Even with all the braking and pushing with each stride, the body and mind start to adapt to the effort it takes to run in this unnatural fashion. Muscles get tighter and the impact increases, the range of motion is decreased, and the running form continues to evolve into something that is far from natural.

It takes time and patience to retrain your body to run naturally. Start by visualizing what natural running form looks like and remembering that we were all born to run. Think about being relaxed and centered with gravity.

The first and most important step in transitioning to natural running is getting your feet under your body mass rather than out in front of your body. Any foot strike that is in front of the body, whether it is at the heel, midfoot, or forefoot, is considered to be a braking moment. As discussed previously, valuable time is lost with the touchdown of the foot in front of the body as the upper body goes from a rear-leaning position to again being centered over that foot. To maintain forward momentum, you must then apply excessive force and push off to start a new stride. That increases vertical up and down movement, which creates fatiguing impact to muscles and joints and sheer forces on the joints and lower back, and strains propulsive muscles, tendons, and connective tissue as you apply power.

Is that how you run? There's an easy way to find out. While you are running, glance down toward your foot strike; if you can see your landing foot at all, you are overstriding. Simply shorten your stride, speed up your cadence, and lean from your center slightly, and you're on the way to natural, efficient form.

A Light Touch

Remember, natural running starts with your feet. Landing lightly under the body at the midfoot/forefoot region of your foot allows you to:

- properly sense the ground, thereby sending your brain the signals it needs to respond appropriately;

- lock the ankle and therefore eliminate excessive rotational forces of the foot and ankle;

- eliminate braking forces and the debilitating impacts, slower cadence, and tight and fatigued muscles associated with a heel-striking gait;

- diminish the impact of the ground with the muscles, tendons, bones, and fascia of the foot, flexed ankle, lower leg, and flexed knee;

- maintain an upright posture with a slight forward lean and a compact arm swing parallel to your body, which contribute to forward propulsion and momentum;

- put yourself in a position to lift your knee to begin a new stride;

- eliminate the inefficient vertical oscillation associated with braking and excessive force of pushing off the ground to start a new stride; and

- run relaxed, both mentally and physically.

Body Position

To get to the starting stance, or "posturing position," of natural running form (see Figure 8.1), you need to start from a position that is centered with gravity. Your knees and ankles should be slightly flexed. Your head should be upright and your eyes should be looking forward. You should have a slight forward lean.

From there, all you need to do is lean slightly forward from your center and lift one foot off the ground to start the motion of running. As you start to fall forward, let that leg drop back to the ground as you lift the other leg. Land lightly under your body with the original leg, sensing the ground, allowing the heel to settle to the ground, and then immediately lift that leg to start a new stride (see Figure 8.1). Continue repeating the process. That quickness ensures a rapid stride cadence, which is important in creating the timing for the rest of your body's movements. Indeed, a 2010 University of Wisconsin study suggests that runners who increase their cadence reduce vertical oscillation, produce lower braking forces, and more often strike the ground close to their center of mass (Heiderscheit 2010). As far as execution, think about running on hot coals: Touch the ground lightly and quickly and get the foot off the ground immediately. Run quietly and smoothly.

Your upper body should be straight from your hips to your shoulders, which will allow you to engage core strength as you lift your knee to start a new stride. Your shoulders should be back and your arms should be held at 90 degrees in a plane parallel to your body, alternately pulling back. Your hands should be relaxed, with your thumb and forefinger touching slightly. Above all, you should have a relaxed mind and body to make the smooth whole-body movements with less effort.

As you lean forward slightly, try to find the sweet spot of balance as your footsteps land lightly under your body. Lift your leg off the ground

| Starting stance | Quick cadence | Land lightly |

Figure **8.1** | *Natural running gait*

with the aid of your hip flexors instead of pushing downward with excessive muscular force from your feet, calves, and hamstrings. Keep your head level and upright and continue looking forward. Feel your elbows alternately pulling backward in time with the opposite foot being lifted off the ground. Shorten your stride and increase your turnover rate, or cadence. Target 180 to 190 strides per minute.

A natural running gait uses the lower body like a spring that reduces both impact and rotational forces. With a "quiet" and upright torso centered over the landing foot, you minimize excessive power output needed during each stride. Your short strides and quick cadence will dictate that you run with a compact arm swing at the same pace. With no braking forces, you'll experience a vast reduction in both vertical oscillation and the need to apply more power to push off after the braking moment.

By that simple act of striking your foot under your body and the actions that follow, you've taken the first steps to a lifetime of healthy running.

Troubleshooting

What happens when you become fatigued? You might be near the end of a long run or race and feel that you want to revert back to heel striking. Don't. Remember the fundamentals and keep plugging. Focus on shortening your stride and ensuring your foot strikes are under your body. You'll thus be able to retain natural running form. Loosen up, breathe easy, and know you're doing it right.

As mentioned previously, two major by-products of heel striking are pushing off hard and overstriding. If you go from heel striking to overstriding and landing on your forefoot and then pushing off hard, you are springing off your toes and will overuse your calf muscles and Achilles tendon. Instead, land lightly at your midfoot/forefoot with your foot parallel to the ground and then lift your knee to begin a new stride.

In many cases, it's easier for severe heel strikers to learn midfoot striking first. (This is the style of running fostered by ChiRunning founder Danny Dreyer.) Landing totally flatfooted and lifting your leg to begin a new stride will safeguard you from landing on your toes and straining your propulsive muscles.

Those who have been practicing midfoot running may want to try landing lightly on the forefoot, allowing the foot to settle and receive the elastic recoil energy return, and then lift off. Forefoot running is a more *performance-oriented* style of running and will provide more speed to a runner when done properly.

Either landing position is correct, because your foot strike is under your mass. Experiment with both midfoot and forefoot styles, but make sure you have a high stride cadence with each style. Land lightly with flexed ankles and knees and immediately lift the knee to begin a new stride, then continue the cycle. As long as you break the habit of pushing off the ground to begin a new stride, you won't be straining your propulsive muscles and tendons, and your running efficiency will improve.

Transition Slowly

Now you know the elements of natural running and how to do it. You can start today, but transition slowly to avoid straining muscles and other soft tissue. During a practical and gradual transition (outlined in Chapter 10), you will engage and strengthen muscles you probably haven't used extensively for running and move in ways your body might not be used to moving. Even if you're very fit and have good core strength, you're bound to be sore or tired during the initial transition phase.

Take your time and relax. Do not try to run too far or fast too soon; just focus on the form and do not overdo it. Be patient; breaking old habits isn't easy. That's why I recommend starting with easy efforts over short distances during which you relentlessly focus on your form. Start by running just 50 meters at a time, exploring what a natural running gait feels like. Once you get the hang of it, gradually ramp up the amount you run—2 miles a couple of times a week, then 4 miles a couple of times a week, and so on. That might not sound like much, but it's the quality of the running—and focusing on running with correct form—that is important, not the quantity. If you're an experienced runner or have a race on the horizon, you don't want to hear someone tell you to back off your mileage. But if you go out and run 5, 10, or 20 miles with a revamped running gait or try to continue your existing training program, you're bound to be sore, or worse, injured. A complete transition might take as few as four to eight weeks for some, but it might take longer for others. Keep in mind that given the benefits, that will seem like a short amount of time.

You might have setbacks in your transition to natural running. At times you'll feel like you're getting it; at other times you won't. You'll have moments of revelation, but then, even though you're doing a lot of things right, you'll suddenly realize you're pushing off to start a new stride or carrying your arms too low. That might make you feel like you're back at square one, but you're not. You're closer than you think, so don't get frustrated. Keep practicing the fundamentals of natural running outlined above, be relentless in the drills, and you'll get there.

9
Dynamic Strength and Form Drills

How can you *improve your running mechanics* and transition to natural running form? I tackle that question in this chapter and the next, with drills and an eight-week training plan to set you on your way to becoming a healthier, more efficient runner. It's easier than you might think, although it does take time. Once you've made the necessary changes, you'll enjoy the benefits for the rest of your life.

The good news is that you're already well on your way. The first step to transitioning to natural running form is understanding it from the biomechanical and physical perspectives outlined in previous chapters. Although the adaptation plans are likely what you're most eager to read and perhaps what compelled you to buy this book, I recommend reviewing previous sections in the book as you begin your personal transition.

In Chapter 10 I detail an eight-week transition plan, but your own transition might take longer; the time needed will vary for everyone. The important thing is that you start now and that you learn to run with natural form properly, eliminating any old bad habits or factors that might inhibit your transition.

The second step in the transition is breaking down the elements of the whole-body kinematics that make up natural running form. The best way to understand the precise individual movements involved in natural running mechanics is through repetitive drills, done primarily in bare feet or less structured shoes. In the beginning, perform these drills in small doses only a couple of times per week so you don't suffer an overuse injury. Do not overdo them. Always err on the side of being patient and conservative in your transition. You may be trying to undo years of running with improper form and perhaps many bad habits developed along the way. In addition, if you've been wearing traditional running shoes with a thick foam midsole and steep heel-to-toe ramp angles, many of the muscles in your feet, ankles, and lower legs have probably been considerably deconditioned, which means you're bound to feel some soreness and fatigue as you reenergize those muscles. That's another reason to listen to your body and avoid over-doing it.

The drills outlined in this chapter are short, meant to stimulate and build muscles, hone the timing of your nervous system, develop proprioception, and create muscle memory. I don't suggest running more than 5 to 10 minutes at a time while barefoot during your first two weeks of transitioning to natural running, especially on natural surfaces.

Speaking of shoes, to achieve optimal natural running form, you'll benefit the most by running in a lightweight, flexible shoe with a low heel-to-toe ramp angle (0 to 5mm) that allows you to sense and engage the ground, sparking the mind–body connection. That's really the only way you'll be able to achieve the proper whole-body kinematics of natural running form. You can run with midfoot/forefoot strikes under your center of mass in thickly cushioned shoes, but the more foam under your foot, the less sensory input will be relayed to your brain.

If you are in a traditional shoe, gradually transition to lighter shoes that allow you to feel the ground before you start running barefoot. By "gradually transition," I mean change shoes immediately but only run very short distances in them. I don't mean alternate back and forth from your old shoes to your new shoes. That will only lengthen your transition and prolong old habits.

Relentless Repetition

As for any athletic endeavor, running requires a lot of muscular strength. There is a false notion that running is a simple sport and that, since you're always tuning up your leg muscles, you really don't need to do ancillary training. Sure, you'll have strong legs if you go out and run five or six times a week. But because natural running form keys on precise whole-body movements and requires core strength (including your hip flexors, upper and lower abdominals, obliques, and psoas), you should constantly work to become universally strong. And, as mentioned previously, your feet might be weak if you've been running with a heel-striking gait in traditional running shoes that don't allow your foot to flex and move the way it would if it were bare.

You must build the necessary strength to properly execute the specific movements of natural running. I have outlined some key strength drills aimed at building the dynamic strength in your core, lower back, feet, ankles, and lower legs. (Note that these are just a starting point; there are dozens of additional drills you can do that help develop a dynamically strong core.) If you do them regularly, you should feel noticeable gains in fine-tuned strength within a few weeks. Being persistent with these exercises on an ongoing basis will ensure you have the general strength you need to execute the precise movements of natural running without relying on other muscle groups to help out. Improved core strength helps disperse the load of keeping your body balanced with gravity by spreading that load appropriately away from your leg muscles. The bottom line is that, combined with a strong aerobic system, a sturdy structural system can help you decrease race times, run better workouts, and recover more quickly.

For example, the stronger your hip flexors, abs, psoas, and oblique muscles are, the easier it will be for you to lift your leg to begin a new stride. The stronger your feet, ankles, and lower legs are, the easier it will be to land lightly and use your flexed knee as a spring to mitigate the impact with the ground. However, if you're weak in your core, you'll have a harder time with those two elements and then be inclined to use your big leg muscles to push off to start a new stride.

As you work on strength, you should also add form drills two to three times weekly to your regimen. Form drills accentuate specific aspects of good form and train your body to repeat those specific movements while you are running. But as mentioned previously, both major and minor form changes take time, so be persistent as you transition and above all make sure you are consistent with strength training and form drills.

Though it might be difficult to quantify optimal natural running form, every runner can and should work regularly on improving running technique based on the various segments of natural running. Not only will it improve your running economy, it will help you be less fatigued and allow you to recover from hard workouts and races more quickly.

Strength Drills

Before starting any strength drills, be sure to warm up with a brisk walk, a mile of light jogging with natural form, or a short jaunt on a treadmill or stationary bike. Start by doing two sets of each drill so your body can adapt to the movements and the dynamic mixture of muscle usage. Once you're comfortable with the movements and feel you're capable of doing more, expand to three sets per sessions. Repeat the drills at least three times per week, taking at least one day off in between each session.

1. Stair Step Drills

With a natural running gait, your body absorbs some of the impact of hitting the ground with a midfoot/forefoot foot strike. The ability to do so relies on the elastic recoil of the plantar fascia, Achilles tendon, and several muscle groups in the foot, ankle, and lower leg, which means you must have strong feet, ankle, and lower-leg muscles. One easy drill to help create the dynamic strength is to balance on the edge of a step at your midfoot with a slightly bent knee (facing upstairs) and flex to lift your heel (and your entire body) upward, keeping your hips level and straightening your leg as you rise. Still balancing on that foot, release the tension and allow the heel to dip below the top plane of the step, keeping your hips level as you return to your starting point with a slightly bent knee. Repeat 10 times on each leg per set.

2. Static Squats

With your back against a wall or a post and your feet far enough from the wall that your lower legs are perpendicular to it (about a foot in distance), slide your back down the wall slowly, controlling the motion with the muscles in your lower back, core, and hips while bending at the knees. Stop just before your knees reach a 90-degree angle and hold this position for 10 seconds. This fine-tunes the full complement of muscles in the quad and hamstring groups. Repeat this squat 3–5 times per workout session. (A similar workout can be done with a Swiss ball placed between the wall and your lower back. In that exercise, you gain additional training by flexing your lower back and glutes as you push backward against the ball.)

3. Pillow Drills

Develop proprioception, balance, and foot and lower leg strength by doing one-legged barefoot squats and balance drills on a thick pillow, couch cushion, or air-filled plastic cushion designed for physical therapy drills. With an unstable surface underfoot, your foot naturally tries to seek out the ground to obtain the efferent feedback your brain uses to tell your body what to do next. These drills simulate the communication process your foot takes part in while wearing a shoe, and they create the sensory interaction that tells your brain how to position the rest of your body.

Single-leg squats

Standing on a pillow with one leg, slowly crouch down into a squat position so that the thigh of your active leg is nearly parallel to the ground. Focus the pressure on your midfoot/forefoot and not your heel. Use your hands to gain balance, keeping them  close to your sides. Keep your head level and focus your eyes ahead. Slowly rise back up, keeping even pressure on your midfoot/forefoot. Repeat 8–10 times per set, adding another set every week.

Squats with object

Standing on a pillow with one leg, slowly crouch down to a squat position and with your opposite hand touch objects placed on the ground around the front side of the pillow, while maintaining balance and the cadence of your squats. (A small, light-  weight object, like a sock or a tennis ball, works well in this drill.)

4. V-Sits

This exercise enhances core strength by building the upper and lower abs as well as the lower back, groin, and hip flexors. From a supine position (belly button pointing upwards) with knees bent, slowly contract your abdominals and lift your legs and upper torso, careful not to lunge with your arms. Stop when your upper torso and legs are angled at approximately 45 degrees in a "V" position. Hold that position for two seconds and then slowly return to the starting position. This helps build the core strength necessary to keep your body balanced with gravity by spreading the load appropriately away from your leg muscles, and this drill ultimately allows you to easily lift your leg to start a new stride. Do 5–10 reps per set.

5. Slow Crunches

From a supine position, your knees bent and your back and feet flat on the ground, slowly raise your head and upper torso while extending your arms low to the ground along your hips and upper legs. The key to this drill is to move slowly and to initially engage the smaller muscles in your upper and lower abs, not just the larger muscles that typically do most of the work. (Quick, jerking movements are facilitated

continued

5. Slow Crunches, continued

by larger muscle groups and should be avoided.) As your head rises, extend the reach of your arms as close to your feet as possible and then return in the opposite direction, moving slowly back to the starting position. This is one of many exercises that develop more complete core strength, which ultimately facilitates lifting a new leg to begin a stride. Start with 5–10 reps per set.

6. Pedestal Exercises

These exercises target and isolate muscle groups from the mid-thigh to the bottom of the rib cage that facilitate the whole-body kinematics of natural running. Ultimately they'll help you build the stable base you need to support the movement of your legs and the positioning of your upper body, especially when you're fatigued.

Prone elbow single-leg raise

From a prone position balancing on the forearms, elbows, and toes, slowly lift one leg upward to almost full rear extension, keeping your toes pointed downward and knees straight. Keep your body aligned in the same plane, from the shoulder to the hips to the ankle of the stationary leg. (Note: Avoid allowing your hips to rise too high.) Repeat 5–10 times on each leg per set.

Supine elbow single-leg raise

From a supine position and balancing on the forearms and elbows and a stationary foot, lift the opposite leg upward to almost full extension, keeping your toes pointed forward and legs only slightly bent. As in the previous exercise, keep your body aligned from shoulders to hips to the ankle of the stationary leg. (Avoid letting your hips droop below the plane created by your shoulders and toes.) Repeat 5–10 times per set.

Lateral elbow single-leg raise

Turned to one side while balancing on the downward elbow, forearm, and stationary foot, raise the opposite foot and leg to almost full upward extension. Rest your upward arm on your hip, pointing the elbow upward while keeping your neck, torso, hips, and legs in the same vertical plane of alignment. Repeat 5–10 times per set and repeat the drill on the other side of your body. (You can do a slightly more difficult variation of the same exercise by balancing your weight on your downward hand with an extended arm.)

Prone flexed-knee elbow hip lift

Balancing on the forearms, elbows and one knee in a prone position with a straight back and rigid core, slowly lift the opposite knee to full upward extension with flexion in the knee. Hold this position for several seconds. Maintaining the same strong posture, slowly return the leg to the starting position. Repeat 5–10 on each leg per set.

Prone flexed-knee balance hip lift

Balancing on the hands and knees, slowly extend your left arm with a straight elbow until it is perpendicular to the ground. Then slowly lift your right leg with a bent knee to full extension, stopping once the upper leg becomes perpendicular to the ground. Hold these extended positions while balancing on the left knee and right hand for 2–3 seconds before slowly returning to the starting position. Repeat 5–10 times on each leg per set.

Supine flexed-knee elbow hip lift

Balancing on the forearms, elbows, and one foot from a supine position with a straight back and rigid core, lift the opposite leg upward with flexion in the knee. Maintaining the same strong posture, slowly return the leg to the starting position. Repeat 10 times per set.

7. Prisoner Squats

Standing with your feet shoulder's width apart, your hands behind your head, and your elbows aligned in a horizontal plane with your chest, hips, and ankles, slowly bend your knees and lower your body downward in that same plane. As you move downward, roll up on to the balls of your feet and balance momentarily at the lowest point before squeezing your glutes, then rise back to the standing position. This drill helps strengthen the lower back, as well as the muscles used in the flexed-knee athletic starting position. Repeat this exercise 10 times per set.

8. Forward Lunges

From a standing position, take a large step forward with one leg. With a straight torso, tight core, and flexed knees, lower your center of mass slowly downward until your back knee is approximately 6–8 inches from the ground. Hold momentarily, then reverse the action and return to the standing position. This exercise engages the core, upper hamstrings, and quads as you go from being in a balanced position to an off-balance position in a simulated one-legged stance. Repeat 5–10 times on each leg per set.

Form Drills

Form drills are easy to do and don't take a lot of time, but they're often overlooked, forgotten, or ignored once a day's workout is completed. Taking an extra 5 to 15 minutes to do form drills several times per week can help your running immensely. You can become more fluid, more efficient, and faster for both short and long distances, assuming you're already training effectively and consistently.

Most drills take one or more aspects of good form—a compact arm swing; soft foot strikes at the midfoot; quick leg turnover (or high cadence of about 180 steps per minute); an upright posture with a slight forward lean at the ankles; a steady but relaxed head, jaw, neck, shoulders, and torso—and accentuate them in a repetitive motion that trains the body to be comfortable with that movement when it is inserted into your typical running mechanics. Some drills are aimed at building smaller muscles (such as the intrinsic group and lumbrical group in the foot), some emphasize midfoot foot strikes under your center of mass, and others help your neuromuscular system to fire more quickly.

Before starting any form drills, warm up with a brisk walk, a mile of light jogging with natural form, or a short jaunt on a treadmill or stationary bike. The drills are broken down into three groups based on how they are introduced in transition to natural running in Chapter 10. Initially, the drills might be your only workout for the day, but eventually you'll do them in conjunction with other drills and/or some type of prescribed running. You can do the drills before or after your running workout, but doing them after a workout can be especially helpful in loosening muscular tightness brought on by intense, repetitive motion from various workout speeds and durations.

Remember, when doing these drills, keep the intensity low and *focus on form.*

Group 1

1. Run in Place

This sounds simple, but it requires an adherence to every aspect of good form mentioned above, only in a semistationary setting while varying your cadence from slow to very high. While you're doing this drill, think about each aspect individually and how each plays into the bigger picture of your running form. This drill is especially effective in teaching your body to increase leg cadence (optimally to 180 steps per minute) and how to lift your leg to start a stride instead of pushing off. Do three 15-second sessions per set.

2. Jump Rope

Jumping rope helps instill soft, mostly flat, midfoot landings and allows elastic recoil as your heel settles on the ground before a new stride begins. (Your body will naturally not let you land on your heel—especially if you're jumping rope barefoot—because landing on your heels would inflict too much force on the bones, muscles, and other tissue in your heels, ankles, and legs.) Jumping rope also reinforces the notion that a new stride should begin by lifting your leg instead of pushing off. As you jump off the ground, focus on lightly lifting your feet off the ground instead of forcefully pushing off the ground. Alter your tempo among slow, medium, and fast speeds, all while concentrating on the tenets of good form. Each set should be 15–20 seconds in duration.

3. High Knees

Running in place with high knees accentuates the need to lift your foot off the ground instead of forcefully pushing off to begin a new stride. This is essentially an act of jogging in place with an overaccentuation on alternately lifting your knees to a 90-degree angle, with your thighs parallel to the ground. (As in the Run in Place drill, your slight forward lean and the momentum gained in this drill will gradually move you forward.) Be sure to focus on soft, relaxed foot strikes, using your core  to lower your leg slowly instead of letting it crash to the ground. This drill requires and also helps instill a compact and consistent arm swing, even though your arms might cycle slightly slower to coincide with the longer hang time of your legs. The motion of your arms will actually help you lift a leg off the ground to start a new stride and keep you balanced. (Briefly try this drill with your arms stationary at your sides. You'll find yourself forcefully pushing your feet off the ground, and you'll have a more difficult time keeping balanced.) Keep your torso, head, and shoulders relaxed and fairly still during this drill and avoid too much vertical oscillation with your center of mass. Each set should consist of alternating high-knee lifts, 10 elevations of each leg.

4. Butt Kicks

Butt kicks accentuate the recovery portion of the running gait phase. Instead of using your hamstring to lift your leg off the ground, think about alternately flicking your lower leg backward with the use of your quadriceps, glutes, and hip flexor muscles and then dropping it back down to the ground under the center of your mass. The movement should be quick and pronounced but relaxed so that you're able to return your foot to the ground softly at the midfoot. As in the high knees drill, a compact and consistent
arm swing is crucial to keeping your balance and maintaining a high cadence. Each set should consist of alternating butt kick strides, 10 elevations of each leg.

Group 2

1. Donkey Kicks

This drill looks just like what it sounds like. With the straight, slightly forward-leaning posture, compact arm swing, level hips, and flexed ankles and knees of the athletic "ready" position, pull one leg backward as if you're kicking something behind

continued

1. Donkey Kicks, continued

you. While balancing on the midfoot area of the stationary leg, repeatedly pull one leg backward and allow it to recoil forward as if it is beginning the recovery phase of the gait cycle. This drill accentuates good hip extension and teaches your body to make foot strikes under your center of mass. Do 10 kicks with each leg per set.

2. Arm Pull Backs

This drill accentuates the motion of the arms during the gait cycle by highlighting primarily the rear portion of the compact arm swing. With a level head, level shoulders, and a straight and slightly forward-leaning running posture, alternate

pushing your arms backward as they are held at 90 degrees (or less). The key is keeping your arms swinging in a plane parallel to your torso and not rotating your shoulders to assist the movement. Do a total of 20 alternate pull backs per set, 10 with each side.

3. Step Overs

This drill emphasizes the motion of lifting your leg off the ground without lunging forward or pushing off the ground with great force. To do this drill, line up a few objects on the ground (such as a hardcover book or a rolled-up sweatshirt). Start striding toward the object, lifting a leg as your body moves forward deliberately and with a consistent arm swing, avoiding contact with each object as you step over it.

4. Body Balance

This drill helps you better recognize and sense a centered and balanced position, so crucial in natural running form. Start the drill by running in place. Now tilt your body forward, noticing that you begin to run forward. After a few steps, return to an upright position, running in place as before. Now tilt your body backward and notice that you begin to move backward. Alternate this forward and backward motion, noting your overall sense of balance.

Group 3

1. Skipping Drills

Quick skipping

The goal of this drill is to quicken the timing of your neuromuscular system so you can increase your running cadence to 180 steps per minute or slightly faster. As you quickly lift one leg off the ground with the start of a stride, the other foot skips off the ground with two small and quick hops before the legs switch roles and do the alternate movement. There is a staccato sensation to this drill when it's done correctly. A compact and very quick arm swing is crucial to keeping your balance and maintaining a high cadence. Each set should consist of about 15–20 seconds of skipping.

Slow skipping

Unlike the previous drill, this is a slow-action skipping drill that accentuates the high knee action of the lifted leg during a running stride. With this drill, you'll practice lifting your leg off the ground to begin a new stride instead of pushing off the ground, and to extend the lifted leg's duration in the air, you'll skip with the opposite foot. The rhythm of this drill will also have a staccato effect, but it will be much slower. A compact but slightly slower arm swing is crucial to keeping your balance and maintaining a high cadence. Each set should consist of about 15–20 seconds of skipping.

2. Acceleration Strides

Any coaches worth the salt in their sweat will recommend doing post-run acceleration strides several times per week. Strides, also called buildups, wind sprints, or striders, allow the body to go through a full range of motion and accentuate every aspect of good form with fast-paced running, especially a high cadence, good hip extension, and a quick, compact arm swing. The keys here are controlled speed while using as little energy as possible, soft foot strikes at the midfoot, and the practice of lifting a leg (and not pushing off the ground) to begin a new stride cycle. Strides should not be all-out sprints, but they should start at a moderate pace and then build up to a fast, fluid effort that's about 75 percent of your top-end speed. Near the end of each stride, taper down the speed to a slow jog and then rest 30 seconds before starting another one. Do 4–6 strides over 50–75 meters in each set to complete exercise.

Barefoot Running: Good in Small Doses

Unless you've been completely out of touch with the world, have no access to various sources of news, and don't talk to anyone on your long weekend runs, you've probably heard about the barefoot running trend. It's been difficult not to, given the proliferation in mainstream media such as the *New York Times*, *Los Angeles Times*, CNN, ABC News, and *Time* magazine.

If done occasionally in small doses, barefoot running helps improve your mechanics and teaches you to land lightly at your midfoot/forefoot, even while wearing shoes. It can strengthen the muscles and fascia in your feet and ankles so you're not relying on the lower and upper leg muscles to do too much work when your foot touches the ground. Remember, when you land at your midfoot/forefoot, your foot flexes, engages the arch, and locks the ankle, then uses your flexed knee as a suspension spring. Running barefoot helps enhance that process by putting you in the proper form and strengthening the muscles that execute those movements.

If you've never done any kind of barefoot drills or running, transition into barefoot exercising slowly. Consider starting with the walking gait, rolling from heel to mid-stance to toe-off and then jogging lightly with natural form. After a few weeks, you can start running easy acceleration strides or a few cooldown laps on the soft grass infield after a long run or track workout.

Virtually all of America's top professional and collegiate distance-running coaches—Alberto Salazar, Terrence Mahon, Greg McMillan, Pete Rea, Greg Barker, Vin Lananna, Karen Harvey, and Jay Johnson, to name a few—utilize some form of barefoot running or barefoot strength and proprioception drills as a means of improving and maintaining a runner's form, preparing for the rigors of racing in lightweight racing flats and spikes, and, ultimately, improving individual running economy to maximize race performance.

However, there are risks to training barefoot, even in small doses, and not everyone is a proponent of it. Take Steve Jones. The former world-record holder in the marathon was a lean, mean running machine in the mid-1980s, as tough and fit and strong as any runner in the world. Today he is a successful marathon coach and does not condone barefoot running, mainly because he doesn't think the rewards outweigh the risks. "There's too much that can go wrong, too many ways to get hurt," he says. What if a runner suffers a bad cut? What if a runner has relatively weak feet or does too much barefoot running too soon and suffers a stress fracture? Those types of injuries, Jones points out, can take you out of training for a full season and perhaps longer.

Jay Johnson coaches several professional middle-distance and distance runners in Boulder, Colorado. He allows runners to run barefoot only a couple of times each week for short durations, about a half-mile at slow speeds on the soft, consistent artificial turf on the infield of the track after a workout. He employs barefoot running as a way to help athletes stretch and relax the foot after a hard workout. It's the slowest running his group of elite runners do all day, and they avoid it when it's too cold, too wet, or too hot.

"We only run barefoot on limited occasions under limited circumstances and, keep in mind, these runners are very fit and very strong," says Johnson.

Johnson also uses several stationary barefoot drills to build proprioception. For example, he'll have athletes balance on one leg or do slow, one-legged squats or lunges with their eyes closed. The brain will still bring the body in balance with gravity, working to overcome the difficulty of not having vision to gauge the surroundings.

What Johnson considers more important to developing strong, nimble feet is running in minimalist shoes. Minimalist shoes, Johnson says, are lightweight and have a relatively flat profile (or low ramp angle) underfoot that allows the foot to land, flex, move, and perform as naturally as it should, with optimally efficient and economical form. This is known as *foot intrinsics.*

"It's the intrinsic ability of the foot to do what it is designed to do, which is absorb shock and move over the ground effectively," Johnson says. "You need that to become a dynamically strong distance runner. But you need to do it wisely."

Focus on Abebe Bikila

Proponents of barefoot running often point to Ethiopia's Abebe Bikila as the patron saint of barefoot runners. He won the 1960 Olympic marathon through the streets of Rome, and vintage photography of a barefooted and determined Bikila is inspiring. But there's more to the story.

Bikila was a late replacement in the 1960 Olympics for injured countryman Wami Biratu, and when he arrived at the Olympic Village to be sized for running shoes supplied by Adidas (which was the footwear sponsor of the Games), he was told they were out of his size and was given a half size smaller. After testing them out in the days leading up to the race, he wasn't comfortable with the fit (remember, how well a shoe fits is a key factor in allowing your feet to control your running) and so decided to run barefoot.

Having run barefoot for much of his life, it wasn't a huge leap for Bikila to consider running without shoes. In 1960, children in rural Ethiopia and Kenya ran (and generally lived) barefoot all the time, often not getting their first pair of shoes until they entered secondary school or got their first job. And while running was a part of their culture—the youth in those cultures ran like American kids played basketball, baseball, or football—the primary surface they ran on was soft, soil or a dirt track, but typically not pavement or asphalt.

So Bikila was prepared. Though running over the large, rounded cobblestones on parts of the Olympic course would be much more challenging than running on smooth concrete surfaces, he had run barefoot on much worse while training to become an imperial guard of Ethiopian emperor Haile Selassie.

Bikila ran barefoot, winning the gold medal in an Olympic record time of 2:15:16. After the race, when asked why he ran barefoot, he deflected the attention from his unshod style to instead honor his country. "I wanted the world to know that my country, Ethiopia, has always won with determination and heroism," he said. The rest is history.

The year after Bikila won Olympic gold, he entered the Mainichi Marathon in Tokyo, Japan. Kihachiro Onitsuka, founder of the Onitsuka Tiger shoe company (later known as ASICS), met Bikila in his hotel and asked him why he didn't bring shoes. When Bikila replied that he didn't have any and planned to run barefoot, Onitsuka cautioned that running barefoot on Japanese roads could be dangerous because of glass, gravel, and other debris. It was certainly a sales pitch for Bikila to try Tiger shoes, but it was grounded in practicality.

As legend has it, Onitsuka raced back to his factory and had his cobblers whip up the lightest pair of running shoes they'd ever made. Bikila wore them the next day, won the race, and never ran a marathon barefoot again. The Ethiopian legend eventually won the 1964 Olympic marathon in Tokyo, becoming the first runner to repeat as champion. He wore a pair of Puma shoes and set a new world and Olympic record of 2:12:11. Bikila continued to run—and win—marathons.

Though Bikila was famous for running a marathon barefoot, a closer look reveals other things about him as a runner. He hadn't worn shoes for most of his life. He had also trained under Onni Niskanen, a leading coach who preached about running with the least effort possible. Watch footage of the 1960 Olympic marathon: Bikila's form looks smooth and effortless, almost as if he was tiptoeing through the streets of Rome. Nobody has perfect running form, but Bikila's was close: His foot strikes were at his midfoot, he had a consistent arm swing to match the high cadence of his legs, his head was upright, and his eyes were focused about 10 meters ahead.

Not surprisingly, his form was virtually identical in the 1964 Olympics, although he was wearing those lightweight Puma shoes. The shoes probably weighed 7 ounces or less, had a very level-to-the-ground profile, and offered protection while still allowing him to feel the ground and let his foot guide his running. If his 1960 victory is held up as a case for running barefoot, then his 1964 race is exhibit A for running with shoes and optimally efficient mechanics.

A Final Word on Barefoot Running

So what should you do? It wouldn't hurt to get your feet screened by a doctor or physical therapist trained in the biomechanics of the foot. Some foot types cannot handle the impacts of barefoot running, such as feet with hypermobility, hypomobility, or imbalances in the forefoot that need correcting by an orthotic. Also, tissue in muscle, tendon, ligament, skin, and the fat pads under your feet can take a long time to adapt to hard impacts, contact with abrasive surfaces, and the full range of motion that occurs when barefoot. Work boots, men's and women's dress shoes, cowboy boots, and many types of sneakers have elevated heels, and that means that for most of us, our feet are used to a limited range of motion, dampened feedback, a layer of protection, and a shortened Achilles tendon. Even small amounts of barefoot running (or walking) can leave feet sore and fatigued, but too much barefoot running can lead to injuries like plantar fasciitis, an inflamed Achilles tendon, or strained calf muscles.

The principle behind barefoot running makes sense. But you can get many of the same benefits in lightweight, minimalist shoes, and they will protect your feet from hazards like glass, gravel, and debris. Wearing shoes also gives you thermal protection properties that are lacking when you run barefoot. Unless you're able to run on the smooth grass of a golf course or a soft, sandy beach, wearing lightweight shoes that allow for barefoot-style running is a more sensible alternative.

The bottom line is that barefoot running should be only one part of your overall training. If you are going to do it, do it responsibly, sensibly, and in small doses at low intensity, allowing the foot and ankle to relax and adapt to the ground.

10

Natural Running
An Eight-Week Transition Plan

I've been helping runners transition to efficient natural running form for more than 20 years. Long before anyone was calling it "natural running," long before anyone was getting notoriety from running barefoot, and long before anyone realized what was wrong with the design of traditional running shoes, I was helping runners understand how and why to land lightly at the midfoot/forefoot region of the foot and how that relays sensory feedback to the brain and ultimately positions the rest of the body in an optimal running posture.

Since the natural running re-evolution exploded, I have conducted running form clinics on a regular basis from the Newton Running Lab in Boulder, Colorado, as well as at numerous retailers, races, and other events around the United States. I am often asked, "Can anyone make the change to natural running form?" My answer is always, "Yes." Anyone can benefit from a transition to a more efficient style of running, even though no two runners are alike. Runners come in all shapes and sizes, and some body types are more suited for running than others. From a physics point of view, it's going to take more force to move more mass over a specific distance. But the main focus for both running performance and reducing the chance for injuries is learning to run more efficiently, no matter your body type, fitness level, or experience as a runner.

The more generally fit you are, the better athlete you'll be, and that will help you considerably in your adaptation to natural running form. Having good core and general strength will help you engage your whole body, not just your legs, while you run. Eating a healthy, well-balanced diet; staying well hydrated; getting plenty of sleep; and developing greater core strength will also go a long way in improving your fitness as a runner. The more you meet your body's needs naturally, the better off you will be.

And remember, whatever you put on your feet has the ability to alter your natural form. I highly recommend that you invest in a pair of shoes conducive to natural running, preferably a lightweight model that allows you to sense the ground, without a chunky, built-up heel. Unfortunately, looks can be deceiving, and most retailers don't readily talk about heel heights or ramp angles. But you should know a shoe with a relatively flat profile when you see one.

Although it might take as little as a month to adjust your stride to a more natural running gait, it could take longer, even up to a year. The time needed is different for everybody, but the rewards are huge, so be patient and know you're on the verge of something great. You need to accept this as a challenge and be diligent in the time and effort you put into it. There are no magic pills or shortcuts to speed you through this transition. You can only proceed at the pace at which your mind and body are able to respond.

I have outlined a fairly conservative eight-week plan in this chapter, knowing that readers are coming to it from various athletic backgrounds, with different running abilities, and thus will have different experiences in their transition. Some might find the transition plan challenging because it is so gradual, with very little running. Others might find the strength and form drills exhausting. No matter what your experience or frustrations are, keep a calm head and remember that the benefits of becoming a healthier, stronger, more efficient runner are long-lasting. Avoid increasing your mileage or running frequency faster than the plan recommends or adding speedwork until you have made a complete transition to natural running form.

You might consider getting a running partner to join you as you begin your transition. Having someone to watch you do your drills and examine your natural form can be like having a personal coach. You can compare ideas and add some fun to the sometimes monotonous experience of doing drills. Also, if you have access to a video camera, have your partner shoot footage of your side view as you run by. Watching the video can be a valuable resource as you self-analyze your form and learn where you need to improve as well as how far you have come.

The order in which you perform the strength and form exercises is not important. What matters most is staying relaxed and focusing on proper form.

The best time to begin a transition to natural running is when you are healthy and uninjured. If you're dealing with an injury, you should let it heal or get treatment for it before starting an ambitious leap into this program. Even something as temporary as a pulled hamstring can affect your ability to make the precise movements of natural running form.

I also highly recommend visiting a foot specialist who can determine your foot type and whether you need forefoot balancing. Starting a transition to natural running without properly addressing forefoot issues could delay your progress and create undue soreness and injury. Be sure whomever you visit—a podiatrist, physical therapist, or footwear specialist—understands the movements of running and the importance of being balanced with gravity.

When it comes to slowly increasing your mileage and training for a race, I highly recommend following the principles of Arthur Lydiard (see Lydiardfoundation.org), the legendary coach from New Zealand who developed tenets of naturally building up the body's systems to handle the rigors of long-distance running. Lydiard stressed developing a big endurance base with high-mileage training that strengthens the aerobic engine. With the help of friend and four-time Olympic marathoner Lorraine Moller, who was coached in the Lydiard ways and cofounded the Lydiard Foundation, I have outlined the primary tenets of Lydiard's training philosophies at the end of this chapter. After you go through my eight-week transition plan, you can add mileage and specific workouts keeping in mind Lydiard's principles.

Transition Plan: Weeks 1–4

Following is a transition plan to natural running form for runners of all abilities. I have included a chart that summarizes each week's activities.

Week 1

Focus for the week: Be relaxed and focus on flexibility and lighter, more graceful (less powerful) running movements.

Running: Up to 10 minutes at a slow, easy pace, every other day.

Drills: Alternate two sets of strength drills and three sets of form drills every other day.

Start your transition slowly and don't expect changes to take place immediately. You won't be doing much running this week. Instead, the primary goal is to spend time doing the strength drills and select form drills detailed in Chapter 9. If you're concerned about losing your aerobic fitness, consider hiking, swimming, cycling, or some other kind of gym fitness instead.

For this first week, do the drills wearing lightweight, minimal-ist running shoes—either lightweight racing flats or a new pair of shoes geared toward natural running. If you transition to barefoot running and drills right away, it might be too much of a shock for deconditioned muscles and soft tissue, and you could wind up sore, or worse, injured. Start with one set of each drill and alternate every other day between strength and form drills. Also start walking around your home barefoot and consider wearing more minimal shoes to work or during leisure time, as they help engage foot and lower leg muscles that have been dormant for years.

Whenever you're beginning any kind of workout or drill session, be sure to warm up your muscles with at least a brisk walk. I also recommend dynamic warm-up drills instead of static stretching. When you're done with your training session, cool down with a relaxed walk followed by light stretching.

For this week's training, you'll be doing a mix of strength drills, specific form drills, and brief running efforts. Complete two sets of strength drills every other day, focusing on slow, precise movements as directed in each drill's description. The form drills you should focus on are running in place,

Training: Week 1

Focus	Relaxed Running Movements
Monday	2 sets strength drills form analysis
Tuesday	3 sets form drills: *jump rope, run in place,* *high knees, butt kicks* 10 min. 100m walk/run repeats
Wednesday	2 sets strength drills
Thursday	3 sets form drills: *jump rope, run in place,* *high knees, butt kicks* 10 min. 100m walk/run repeats
Friday	2 sets strength drills
Saturday	3 sets form drills: *jump rope, run in place,* *high knees, butt kicks* 10 min. 100m walk/run repeats
Sunday	2 sets strength drills

high knees, butt kicks, and jump rope. The key is to do them with precision but in a relaxed manner that doesn't entail too much muscular force. With each drill, you will be working on aspects of the optimal running form discussed in Chapter 8. With the running in place drill, focus primarily on touching the ground lightly and then lifting your leg with your core and hip flexors to begin a new stride. The drills recommended for this week are all variations of one-legged stance drills (even the two-footed jump rope drill) and can give you an idea of what it feels like to be balanced at the hips and interacting with the ground with a midfoot/forefoot foot strike. With the butt kicks and high knees drills, think about lifting your leg lightly and then letting the other one drop easily to the ground with a light landing. With the jump rope drill, think about being light on your feet, land on your forefoot with flexed knees, and focus on relaxed ankles and lower leg muscles.

Occasionally, start a slow, easy jog with natural running form between drills and experience how parts of those particular drills feel in relation to the whole-body movements of your revised running form. Remember how that feels and how different it is from a heel-striking gait.

For your running workouts this week, run the straightaway of a track and walk the curves. Run at a slow, very easy pace for 10 minutes total, focusing on relaxed, graceful movements of natural running. If a local track isn't accessible, run on a dirt trail or in a grassy park.

Avoid running more than 10 minutes at any given time during this first week. Pushing forward with longer runs before you grasp good form will be detrimental to your progress. Be honest with yourself about your progress, and don't get upset if you feel awkward and clumsy at times. That's bound to happen as you try to put your body into positions it's not used to, just as if you were taking golf, tennis, or snowboarding lessons.

Frequently examine your posture by running in place in front of a full-length mirror. See what the proper movements look like, but also look for things you're not yet executing correctly and determine if you can fix them by breaking down the specific movements while looking in the mirror. Do you have good posture? Are your shoulders and hips level? Is your upper torso upright and leaning slightly forward when you run? Answering these types of questions and making adjustments will help you in your transition.

Week 2

Focus for the week: Balance and forward lean

Running: Up to 15 minutes at a slow, easy pace every other day.

Drills: Alternate two sets of strength drills and three sets of form drills every other day.

In addition to practicing light, graceful movements and foot strikes, focus closely this week on balance and forward lean and how each plays a roll in overall natural running mechanics. Keep doing the strength drills and the form drills you started in the first week (still while wearing lightweight shoes) and add arm pull back, step over, donkey kick, and body balance drills to your repertoire. When doing those drills, think about how each

Training: Week 2

Focus	Balance and Forward Lean
Monday	3 sets form drills: *jump rope, run in place,* *high knees, butt kicks,* *arm pull backs, body balance,* *step overs, donkey kicks* 15 min. easy run
Tuesday	2 sets strength drills
Wednesday	3 sets form drills: *jump rope, run in place,* *high knees, butt kicks,* *arm pull backs, body balance,* *step overs, donkey kicks* 15 min. 100m walk/run repeats
Thursday	2 sets strength drills
Friday	3 sets form drills: *jump rope, run in place,* *high knees, butt kicks,* *arm pull backs, body balance,* *step overs, donkey kicks* 15 min. easy run
Saturday	2 sets strength drills
Sunday	3 sets form drills: *jump rope, run in place,* *high knees, butt kicks,* *arm pull backs, body balance,* *step overs, donkey kicks* 15 min. easy run

is affected by a slightly forward lean and how your body is balanced with gravity. Alternate doing two sets of strength drills and three sets of form drills every other day, while also adding in 15 minutes of running up to four times per week.

On day one this week, run 5 minutes slowly in your new lightweight shoes built for natural running, then run 5 minutes barefoot on a soft surface, followed by 5 more minutes in shoes. (Be careful where you run barefoot. Consider running on the infield of a local high school track, on the soft grass of a park, or along a sandy beach.) As you run, think about the key points of natural running form both while wearing shoes and in bare feet. Think about how you automatically balance your body with gravity in each situation. Pick up on cues of how perfect your form is while barefoot and try to mimic those sensations and movements while wearing shoes. While running, remember to (1) land lightly with your midfoot/forefoot under your body mass and immediately start a new stride by lifting that leg up; (2) have a slight forward lean while keeping your hips and shoulders square; (3) maintain a compact arm swing close to your body with your elbows at 90 degrees; and (4) keep your head upright with your eyes looking to the horizon.

Run up to 15 minutes at a time every other day. Don't worry about how far or how fast you're running; focus only on form. Stop as much as necessary during the run to self-examine your form. Back off from running if you wake up overly sore one day. Soreness can come from engaging dormant muscles, but it can also come from strained muscles. It's a fine line, but it's important to try to understand the difference. This also might be a good time to get a professional therapeutic massage or invest in self-massage tools to relieve some of the tightness.

When you're running, the most important thing you should be doing is landing lightly at the midfoot/forefoot and letting your heel settle. A common mistake is landing on the toes. By doing so, you're running in a modified sprinting gait and likely pushing off the ground fairly hard to start a new stride, which is bound to lead to tight, sore calf muscles and a tight Achilles tendon.

Week 3

Focus for the week: Think about being quick and light by picking up the cadence of your running and your form drill sessions.

Running: Up to 20 minutes every other day.

Drills: Alternate every other day with two sets of strength drills and three sets of form drills.

By now you should be starting to get a feel for how natural running form comes together. But you're also likely eager to run more. Restrain the urge to do anything more than what is prescribed, and you'll benefit in the long

Training: Week 3

Focus	Quick and Light Cadence
Monday	2 sets strength drills
Tuesday	3 sets form drills: *jump rope, run in place,* *high knees, butt kicks,* *arm pull backs, body balance,* *step overs, donkey kicks,* *skipping drills, strides* 20 min. 100m walk/run repeat
Wednesday	2 sets strength drills
Thursday	3 sets form drills: *jump rope, run in place,* *high knees, butt kicks,* *arm pull backs, body balance,* *step overs, donkey kicks,* *skipping drills, strides* 20 min. easy run
Friday	2 sets strength drills
Saturday	3 sets form drills: *jump rope, run in place,* *high knees, butt kicks,* *arm pull backs, body balance,* *step overs, donkey kicks,* *skipping drills, strides* 20 min. easy run
Sunday	2 sets strength drills

run. Think about how far you've come and don't worry if you're finding your transition to be slow and challenging. A complete transition will take time. There are still plenty of microadjustments to make before you start to log longer runs and harder workouts.

This week, continue with two sets of strength drills (add a third if you feel ready) and add skipping quickly, skipping slowly, and acceleration strides to your repertoire of form drills. These drills are specifically designed to retrain the timing of your nervous system and increase your stride cadence. Think about being quick and light with every step and movement, allowing that to carry over to every drill you do. You can add a set of form drills while barefoot a couple of times a week, but make sure you're doing those drills on a soft surface.

For your running this week, do two slow, easy 20-minute runs in your light-weight natural running shoes and the "straights and turns" track workout from previous weeks. Use the increased cadence of your drill sessions to increase the quickness and cadence of your running form. This doesn't mean you should run faster; in fact, you should not. It means you should increase the frequency of your leg turnover and try to approach 180 steps per minute. Test yourself by counting your steps for a full minute or do an abbreviated test by counting only your right foot strikes and see if you reach at least 23 in 15 seconds or 45 in 30 seconds. Stop often during your 20-minute runs to make minor form adjustments and ensure you maintain quick leg turnover.

As you run, ask yourself questions to prompt proper movements. Are your feet landing lightly on the ground under your center of mass? Are your knees and ankles slightly flexed when your foot hits the ground? Are your arms at 90 degrees and alternately pulling back in unison with the cadence of your legs? Is your head level, with your eyes looking out in front of you? Are you lifting your leg to start a new stride rather than forcefully pushing off? Perhaps most important, is your body relaxed? Is your mind relaxed? Being relaxed is crucial to running with natural form.

Week 4

Focus for the week: This week you can start to put it all together, focusing on the mind–body connection that is integral to the proper mechanics of efficient natural running form.

Drills: Alternate with three sets of strength drills and three sets of form drills every other day.

Running: Up to 25 minutes, four times per week.

Running naturally requires a synergistic mind–body connection. I'm not talking about some kind of new age meditation, but rather the simple concept of having your mind and body working in unison to properly position and move your body as you run. It's about getting in touch with your body and opening the feedback channels to the brain. It's about

Training: Week 4

Focus	Mind–Body Connection
Monday	3 sets all form drills 25 min. up/down run
Tuesday	3 sets strength drills
Wednesday	3 sets all form drills 25 min. easy run
Thursday	3 sets strength drills
Friday	3 sets all form drills 25 min. up/down run
Saturday	3 sets strength drills
Sunday	3 sets all form drills 25 min. easy run

becoming more athletic and more agile in how you move, taking control of your body, and engaging the proper muscles to move your body as efficiently and naturally as possible. It's about using that sensory feedback to run fluidly, springy and light on your feet, instead of running awkwardly and lumbering like a robot. In other words, don't be brain dead while you run. Be cognizant of your body's movements, how those movements are made in concert with other movements, and how those coordinated movements play a role in rebalancing your body on every stride.

Remember, the mind–body connection doesn't come from being mentally tough and grinding through fatigue in a workout or race. It comes from developing and utilizing the sensory input derived from the foot's interaction with the ground. The result is the smooth, relaxed movements of whole-body kine-matics, not the stressful, power-based movements of a heel-striking gait.

Continue with three sets of strength drills and three complete sets of form drills every other day. As you do the form drills, think about how far you have come in four weeks. Chances are you've started to hone your mind–body connection without thinking about it. When you first started doing the drills, you might have felt clumsy and awkward. By now you should at least feel comfortably fluid with the movements of each of the drills as you start to make use of the sensory feedback you're getting from your quick and light midfoot/forefoot foot strikes.

This is the week when you really start to pull everything together while you run. Consider the mind–body connection when you're running and how it comes naturally when you're running with a high cadence and landing lightly with midfoot/forefoot foot strikes. Make sure you are lifting your leg with your core muscles and hip flexors and not pushing off the ground with force to start a new stride. If you feel fatigued at any point during your running and feel like your form is falling apart or your posture is starting to slack off, make a conscious effort to snap out of it and get back to natural running form. Former Ironman champion Scott Tinley told me he would purposely drop his shoulders and arms, take a few deep breaths, and then reset his posture into proper, upright forward-moving form.

Err on the side of shorter runs if you're still struggling to get your form dialed in. You're not doing yourself any favors if you run longer and revert back to habits of your old form. Control any urge to crank out a 10-miler in your new shoes. You certainly could do it, but you're likely to fall back into those old habits or overuse muscles you haven't used much for running.

This is a good time to have your form captured on video again. Compare that to the footage you took prior to starting your transition plan; you should be pleasantly amazed at the progress you've made. But look at the new video carefully and see if there are things that still need improving. Are you carrying your arms close to your body at about a 90-degree angle, swinging them with a relaxed movement? Is your foot landing under your mass lightly? Do you need to reduce vertical bounce while you run? Remember the things you looked at during the mirror drill and see if those have improved in the video. If there are things you think you should work on, consider doing some of the drills that address that problem at the end of a run, during a cooldown session.

Transition Plan: The Next Steps

Few runners will make a complete transition to natural running after just four weeks. Some people can make minor adjustments and achieve a total transition in a few weeks, but for others it could take as long as a year. Although you've become familiar with the motions of natural running, they haven't been engrained in your muscle memory yet. That's why it's important to remain vigilant with your strength and form drills to build on the progress and investment you've already made.

For the next four weeks, fine-tune your natural running mechanics, continue with strength and form drills, and slowly increase the distance and frequency of your runs. As long as you are not battling lingering soreness or pain, you can increase your mileage gradually and slowly increase the frequency of your runs to about five days a week. However, I highly recommend rest days as well. Your body needs time to recover and repair itself from the rigors that accompany muscular growth and the fatigue of training.

Now that you're more than a month into your transition, you might have a tendency to take your half-finished form out for a 10- to 15-mile run. Your inner marathoner might be craving the unique mix of peacefulness, challenge, and rejuvenation that a long run always brings, but I recommend refraining from going on long runs without a gradual progression. Instead, increase the mileage of your long run by no more than 10 percent per week and make sure you're diligent about self-analyzing your form. The 10 percent rule also applies to your overall weekly mileage.

Picking Up the Pace

We all have different reasons for running, but many of us like to test our fitness and speed by racing. It's fun to race, and you're going to be inclined to find a race and give your revamped running form a whirl. But I don't recommend starting a 12- to 24-week half-marathon or marathon buildup program until you have become completely proficient at natural running. Instead, once you're proficient in the technique, begin with a shorter race distance, such as a 10K, and let that be your gateway back into racing.

Training: Week 5

Monday	Rest
Tuesday	3 sets form drills 25 min. up/down run
Wednesday	3 sets strength drills 3 sets form drills 20 min. easy run
Thursday	2 sets form drills 30 min. easy run
Friday	3 sets strength drills 3 sets form drills cross-training
Saturday	40 min. easy run
Sunday	3 sets strength drills 30 min. easy run

Training: Week 6

Monday	Rest
Tuesday	3 sets form drills 15 min. tempo run
Wednesday	3 sets strength drills 3 sets form drills 20 min. easy run
Thursday	2 sets form drills 30 min. easy run
Friday	3 sets strength drills 3 sets form drills cross-training
Saturday	form drills 30 min. up/down run
Sunday	3 sets strength drills 30 min. easy run

Training: Week 7

Monday	Rest
Tuesday	3 sets form drills 25 min. fartlek run
Wednesday	3 sets strength drills 3 sets form drills 20 min. easy run
Thursday	2 sets form drills 30 min. easy run
Friday	3 sets strength drills 3 sets form drills cross-training
Saturday	45 min. easy run
Sunday	3 sets strength drills 30 min. up/down run

Training: Week 8

Monday	Rest
Tuesday	3 sets form drills 20 min. tempo run
Wednesday	3 sets strength drills 3 sets form drills 20 min. easy run
Thursday	2 sets form drills 30 min. easy run
Friday	3 sets strength drills 3 sets form drills cross-training
Saturday	45 min. easy run
Sunday	3 sets strength drills 35 min. fartlek run

You should continue building your aerobic fitness and start to increase the intensity of your workouts. With all types of workouts, no matter the pace, make sure you're utilizing your mind–body connection and not reverting back to bad habits. One common mistake with a faster workout is the tendency to use more muscular force to push off the ground to begin a new stride. But the real key to running faster is increasing your stride cadence and the lift of your leg during every stride.

In the charts for Weeks 5–8 I include a sample plan to increase your fitness and continue your transition to natural running. It's essentially a way to extend what you have learned during your transition weeks. At the end of this next four weeks, you should be ready to embark on a 10K training plan.

Including faster workouts such as up/down runs, tempo runs, and fartlek runs will add to your overall fitness base, but be careful not to do too much too soon. (For that reason, I'm not including short- and fast-track intervals in this plan.)

You will continue doing strength and form drills throughout this next phase of training. It is only through relentless repetition that you'll develop muscle memory and further your transition to natural running. The chart is just a guideline, and you can vary it so that it makes sense for your schedule. Try to spread out the days on which you do strength and form drills and avoid doing faster workouts on back-to-back days. Also, make sure you build rest days into your weekly regimen. That means 1 or 2 days a week in which you don't run at all, although you can do some sort of cross-training (swimming, cycling, gym fitness) if you wish. But remember, your body needs time to recover and rebuild to compensate for all the stresses of training you inflict on it.

Types of Workouts

Easy Run

After warming up, run consistently somewhere at Zone 1 pace. This is a slow pace that helps a runner recover and starts to build aerobic endurance. This is the easiest type of run to monitor your natural running mechanics, but also the easiest from which to revert back to inefficient heel-striking habits. Focus on running slowly with light foot strikes at your midfoot/forefoot and a quick stride cadence and arm swing, and whole-body natural running kinematics will fall into place.

Up/Down Run

After warming up, run the first portion of the run at a slow, easy pace, or Zone 1. Then for 3 minutes quicken the pace slightly to tempo pace or somewhere in Zone 2 or 3, followed by another segment of slow, easy running for the same duration as the first segment. Think about shifting gears to run slightly faster for that middle segment, making sure to maintain natural running form. (For example, a 25-minute up/down run might be broken down as 11 minutes of slow, easy running, 3 minutes of running at tempo pace, and 11 minutes of easy slow, easy running.)

Fartlek Run

After warming up, alternate your running pace with short but equal segments of slow, recovery pace (Zone 1) and anaerobic threshold pace (Zone 3). You can

Running Paces

Zone 1: Recovery pace

A very slow pace that could be sustained for 3 to 5 hours or longer. It is typically the pace used for warming up, recovery runs, and cooling down. This is a pace at which your heart rate will be at roughly 60 to 70 percent of your maximum with a perceived exertion of 2–5 on a scale of 10.

Zone 2: Aerobic training pace

A moderate pace that can be sustained for up to 2 hours. This training pace improves your aerobic condition, allowing you to run longer distances. This is a pace at which your heart rate will be at roughly 70 to 80 percent of your maximum with a perceived exertion of 5–7 on a scale of 10.

Zone 3: Anaerobic threshold pace

A quick pace that can be sustained for 60 seconds to a few minutes. This pace increases speed endurance, allowing you to run faster once you have a solid aerobic base. This is a pace at which your heart rate will be at roughly 80 to 90 percent of your maximum with a perceived exertion of 7–9 on a scale of 10.

Zone 4: VO$_2$max pace

A very fast pace that can only be sustained for very short periods of time, varying between 10 and 60 seconds. This is a pace at which your heart rate will be at roughly 90 to 100 percent of your maximum with a perceived exertion of 9–10 on a scale of 10.

run the same duration for each segment (such as 2 minutes "on," followed by 2 minutes "off") or vary the efforts between 1 and 3 minutes in length, just as long as the duration of the faster segments matches that of the slower segments.

Tempo Run

A tempo run is a longer fast workout done at a moderately fast pace, typically between Zone 2 and Zone 3. After warming up, run moderately hard at tempo pace for the prescribed duration of time. As with other fast workouts, be sure to maintain natural running form and avoid pushing off the ground with excessive muscular force to begin a new stride.

Heart Rate Training Zones

There are many ways to determine your heart rate training zones, but the easiest is using a formula that estimates your maximum heart rate. Estimation formulas have varied through the years, but as of 2010 the most widely accepted is as follows:

- Males: 210 – 1/2 your age – 5% of your body weight + 4
- Females: 210 – 1/2 your age – 1% of your body weight + 0

For example, if you're a 40-year-old male and weigh 150 pounds, your formula would be as follows:

$$210 - 20 \, (50\% \times 40 \text{ years}) - 7.5 + 4 \text{ (male)} =$$
$$\text{max heart rate of 186.5 beats per minute}$$

What's Next?

After eight weeks, you may or may not need more work to continue your transition to natural running. Even if you have become fairly efficient, you'll still need to continue reinforcing what you've learned for the rest of your life, no different than a golfer working on her golf swing or a pianist practicing playing the piano. At the very least, continue executing strength and form drills several times every week as you begin to increase your mileage during your next buildup to a race.

So how do you know if you need more work? Compare your form while running with shoes to running barefoot on safe surfaces. Do you feel the same sensations while running in shoes as you do while running barefoot? Listen to your body. Is one particular muscle group or soft tissue group overly fatigued or sore on a regular basis? Do you feel like you're landing lightly and lifting off lightly with every stride? Or do you feel like you're still pushing off with excessive muscular force?

At any point that you feel confused or stalled in your progress, review what you've learned about the biomechanics of your feet, the physics of natural running, and optimal running form. Remember, a significant mind–body connection has to occur to facilitate this transition. You need to unlearn habits that have been with you for a long time and retrain your body to run as you did when you were a child. With dedication to the principles of natural running and relentless repetition of strength and form drills, you can progress in your transition to becoming a more efficient, natural runner. But even as you start to master

Refining Your Form

Flaw	Fix
Overstriding	Shorten steps, increase cadence, lean forward.
Landing in front of center of mass/braking	Land under center.
Landing on toes or pointing toes down	Land on midfoot or forefoot/ball of foot.
Pushing off toes with excessive force	Lift and then place foot under your body.
Heel striking	Land under center, shorten stride, increase cadence.
Feet pointed out or pigeon-toed	Feet should point in a forward direction.
Side to side movement, e.g., arms or hips	Make all body movements front to back.
Too much vertical motion	Use higher cadence, shorter strides, lean forward.
Looking down	Look forward to the horizon.
Landing with loud foot strikes	Land lightly and quietly, self-regulate your impact.

natural running, your work isn't done. Like the specific techniques of any sport, becoming an efficient runner takes practice, dynamic strength, and proper training.

The Lydiard Way

The late Arthur Lydiard was the world's original natural running coach. The legendary middle-distance and distance-running coach from New Zealand optimized a runner's fitness by developing the body's natural energy systems gradually and sequentially through periodization to reach a peak period at a specific date (a race), while also giving sufficient attention to rest and recovery. No other distance-running coach in the world has as many ardent followers as Lydiard. Virtually every top-level coach and long-distance runner has used some of his basic principles as the basis for training modern runners for races, from 800m to the marathon. The beauty of Lydiard's training is that it applies to runners of all abilities, from the world-class elite to middle-of-the-packers to those bringing up the rear, just trying to finish.

Lydiard's training system starts by creating a large endurance base, in which the body's aerobic engine is developed by running long and slow over increasing distances. After the base comes strength from hill running and speed from interval training. His system stresses the idea of feeling-based training, in which runners tap into their intuitive "inner coach" to gauge their speed and efforts in various workouts. His runners in the 1950s and 1960s wore shoes that were light and flexible but with almost no support or cushioning, partially because that's what was available at the time, but also because it allowed them to run with natural form and develop their ability to sense the ground and regulate impact and speed.

In the following section, I outline the five essential principles of Lydiard training developed by four-time Olympic marathoner Lorraine Moller, who trained under Lydiard's philosophies and later cofounded the Lydiard Foundation. (For more about Lydiard training programs, go to www.go2lydiard.com.)

Principle I: Maximize Aerobic Capacity

Arthur Lydiard understood that for any running event that lasts longer than about a minute, a runner utilizes energy derived from his or her aerobic system. That's why the development of that system (primarily through comfortably paced sustainable running within the aerobic zone) is the bottom layer of Lydiard's training pyramid, the endurance base on which all other training is built. Developing the aerobic system expands the oxygen-carrying infrastructure of the body—lungs, heart, and the entire respiratory and circulatory systems—and naturally expands the ability to run longer and, eventually, faster.

The greater your aerobic infrastructure—and thus the greater your ability to utilize oxygen—the greater basis you have on which to train, recover, and race efficiently and effectively. In simple terms, the more you run, the more you build your aerobic capacity (although a potential limiting factor is the increased chance for overuse injury). After you have developed that base, you can add strength, speed training, and event-specific sharpening, which are all outlined in subsequent principles. Lydiard preached, "The greater the base, the higher the peak," which is to say that the path to reaching new levels of endurance running must start with a very large base of aerobic conditioning. With a large aerobic base, you can do the harder and more intense workouts, and ultimately, with proper recovery, you'll be able to run faster. "In other words, more oxygen uptake = more energy = greater sustained performance," Moller says.

Your aerobic base can be developed at the start of a training program, and you can continue to develop it over the course of many years. Conversely, no matter how much you train your anaerobic system, once you reach your limits, you can't continue to push the envelope because your ability to tolerate lactic acid won't expand. That's what makes development of the aerobic system key for any level of runner. If you have limited time to train for a 10K, half-marathon, or marathon, you will benefit most if you work on aerobic development by running medium to long distances in the aerobic zone.

Principle II: Feeling-Based Training

Feeling-based training is the ability to accurately read your body's own natural signals to get the most out of your training and racing. Training guru and running author George Sheehan used to say that training for a race is an experiment of one. There are a lot of ways to train, but you need to find out what works for your physical makeup, and that means you must be able to read what your body is telling you so that you can train and recover properly.

Today, runners have dozens of different kinds of tools to help monitor their training, including stopwatches, heart rate monitors, and GPS devices that track speed and distance. Moller advises using those tools as training wheels but warns that you should be careful not to develop a dependence on them. The multitude of information they provide may supplant your feeling-based capability of understanding what your body is naturally telling you. Instead of running yourself into the ground (or, conversely, running too slowly) based on what the data say, you are better off ignoring those devices and listening to the language of your own physiology.

Any good coach will tell you to develop your internal wisdom through mindful engagement with your body. Have you recovered, or do you feel sluggish and fatigued? Are you able to run easily at a given pace, or are you struggling? Lydiard used to prescribe some training runs at half or three-quarter effort, leaving it up to the runner to know and understand what that feels like. "It takes a while, but as runners create a rapport with their bodies and understand their physiology like an inner coach, they will be able to train, recover, and race much more effectively," Moller says. "There's no such thing as a one-size-fits-all program. You have to use your inner coach to do what's right for you."

Principle III: Response-Regulated Adaptation

Arthur Lydiard knew that for every stress inflicted on the body in training, adequate recovery time was necessary for the proper training effect to take place. That's because our physiological development doesn't occur while we're training, but while we're resting. And that means that no matter how fit you are, you cannot follow an absolute "more is better" mantra and expect to improve your performance. You have to find a balance between training and recovery.

Response-regulated adaptation is a way to create that balance, helping you to monitor your response to training and to adjust accordingly. It involves challenging the body with the stress of a workout, allowing the body to recover sufficiently, determining how the body responds, and then adapting your training from there. If you apply another challenge of stress to the body before it's ready, it will be counterproductive to your development. It's a feeling-based process, so you need to learn how to read those signals. Have I recovered? Am I fatigued? Am I ready to stress the body again? Did I get the most out of the last workout? As with feeling-based training, there is a learning curve associated with response-regulated adaptation. Tracking your resting pulse the moment you wake up is one simple recovery indicator tool you can use to determine whether you're fully recovered, but as you get more in tune with your body's natural rhythms, you'll be able to intrinsically sense whether you need more rest or you are ready for a hard workout.

"Once I got in tune with my own physiology, I was never afraid to take time off and let my body come back from injury or after a hard race," Moller says. "It can be dangerous to think, 'The harder I work, the more I'll get out of it,' because that can lead to overtraining or underrecovering. You need to find balance for your body, and that's what this principle stresses."

Principle IV: Sequential Development of Energy Systems

In the Lydiard pyramid training model, each segment builds on the preceding segment, and as you progress up the pyramid, different phases with more intense types of stimuli are applied. Only through the progressive development of the body's energy systems can you reach the maximum performance at the top of the pyramid. You start with aerobic development over a period of time, but after a while your body gets used to that kind of training and your rate of improvement starts to flatten out. That's when your body is ready for the next phase, which in Lydiard training is four to six weeks of strength training derived from hill workouts. From there, your body will be well conditioned to move into four to six weeks of anaerobic development through interval training. Then you can begin to fine-tune your fitness with speedwork geared for a specific event, whether it's an 800-meter race or a 26.2-mile marathon. The final step is known as coordination, which entails filling in the gaps with race-prep time trials. During that phase, you can listen to your body to determine whether you need a few more speed workouts or a few more endurance workouts to round out your training. "Each phase is equally important if you want to reach maximum performance," Moller says. "Lydiard would often say that you'd never want to eat a cake half baked. Nor would you want to run a race with half-baked training."

Principle V: Timing Is Everything

The success of any training program is guiding a runner to the top of the pyramid and providing an opportunity for a peak performance. Whether an athlete achieves optimal performance on race day depends on numerous variables, but having the opportunity to reach that level of performance won't happen without proper timing and sequencing of each phase of training. Lydiard's concept of sequential training is based on what is commonly referred to as periodization, or the notion of doing the correct type of training at the correct time to properly develop and fine-tune a runner's ability as he or she approaches race day. Too much or too little of one kind of training or the right amount at the wrong time can lead to overtraining, underrecovery, and less-than-satisfactory results. Ultimately, the beauty of the Lydiard pyramid approach is that workout programs are written backward, from the intended race day to the start of the base-building phase, allotting the correct amount of time necessary for each phase. Plus, this method helps to sharpen an athlete's mental outlook by creating a definitive focal point that can be visualized and understood from any point during the training program.

A Lifetime of Natural Running

You probably picked up this book intrigued by the idea of becoming a stronger, more efficient runner who is less prone to overuse injuries. Some of the concepts tied to a dramatic change in your running form might have sounded foreign and even radical at first. But by now it should be clear that natural running is actually a simple and intuitive concept, which makes complete sense the moment you step out of your traditionally built running shoes and run barefoot over any surface or in lightweight shoes that promote a midfoot/forefoot gait.

Adopting natural running isn't difficult, but it takes focus and a commitment to replacing old habits with new ones. Understanding and improving your running mechanics, wearing lightweight training shoes that are better suited for a natural running gait, and working continually on building and maintaining strength and technique with drills are all part of the process of becoming an informed runner and therefore a better one.

The good news is that the transition to natural running can begin immediately, and the results last a lifetime. It will take time and adherence to detail, but you *will* become a stronger, healthier, and quite possibly faster runner. More than that, you will tap into a renewed enthusiasm and joy that may be missing in your running. So have patience. Once you learn to run naturally, you'll put yourself in a position to run faster and healthier, not just for today, but for the rest of your life.

Resources

References

Balk, Malcolm. 2009. *Master the Art of Running*. London: Collins & Brown.

Boston Athletic Association (BAA). n.d. bostonmarathon.org.

Christie, Pattie. 2009/2010. Telephone interviews by Danny Abshire and Brian Metzler.

Cucuzzella, Mark. 2009/2010. Telephone and personal interviews by Brian Metzler. Boulder, CO.

Cucuzzella, Mark, and West Virginia University. 2007. ChiRunning Survey. www.chirunning.com.

De Wit, Brigit, et al. 2000. Biomechanical analysis of the stance phase during barefoot and shod running. *Journal of Biomechanics* 33: 269–78.

Dicharry, Jay. 2009/2010. Telephone and personal interviews by Brian Metzler. Boulder, CO.

Dreyer, Danny. 2009. Interview by Brian Metzler. December.

Hartner, Chris. 2009/2010. Telephone and personal interviews by Brian Metzler.

Hasegawa, Hiroshi, T. Yamauchi, W. J. Kraemer. 2007. Foot strike patterns of runners at 15-km point during an elite-level marathon. *Journal of Strength Conditioning Research* 21 (3): 888–893.

Heiderscheit, Bryan C. 2010. Effects of step rate manipulation on joint mechanics during running. *Medicine & Science in Sport & Exercise* 56–59.

Kerrigan, D. Casey, Jason R. Franz, Geoffrey S. Keenan, Jay Dicharry, Ugo Della Croce, and Robert P. Wilder. 2009. The effect of running shoes on lower extremity joint torques. *Physical Medicine and Rehabilitation* 1 (12): 1058–63.

Lieberman, D. E., M. Venkadesan, W. A. Werbel, A. I. Daoud, S. D'Andrea, I. S. Davis, R. O. Mang'eni, and Y. Pitsiladis. 2010. Foot strike patterns and collision forces in habitually barefoot versus shod runners. *Nature* 463: 531–35.

McDougall, Christopher. 2009. *Born to Run: A Hidden Tribe, Superathletes, and the Greatest Race the World Has Never Seen.* New York: Knopf.

Moller, Lorraine. 2010. Telephone interview by Brian Metzler.

New York Road Runners (NYRR). n.d. nyrr.org.

Robbins, S. E., et al. 1987. Running-related injury prevention through barefoot adaptations. *Medicine & Science in Sports & Exercise* 19: 148–46.

Roberts, Amy. n.d. Abstract of unpublished study. Newtonrunning.com.

Rodgers, Charlie. 2010. Telephone interview by Brian Metzler. May 7.

Running USA. 2010 Marathon, Half Marathon and State of the Sport Report. www.runningusa.org.

Ryan, Michael B., Gordon A Valiant, Kymberly McDonald, and Jack E Taunton. 2010. The effect of three different levels of footwear stability on pain outcomes in women runners: A randomised control trial. *British Journal of Sports Medicine* (June). http://bjsm.bmj.com/content/early/2010/06/26/bjsm.2009.069849.abstract?sid=6f514a1a-667b-444d-8689-e6bd8d7ca4ab.

Shorter, Frank. 2010. Telephone interview by Brian Metzler. May 3.

Sports Goods Manufacturers Association (SGMA). 2010. *2010 SGMA Sports & Fitness Participation Topline Report.* www.sgma.com/reports.

Squadrone, R., and C. Gallozzi. 2010. Biomechanical and physiological comparison of barefoot and two shod conditions in experienced barefoot runners. *The Journal of Sports Medicine and Physical Fitness* 49 (1): 6–13.

Stefanyshyn, D. J., et al. 2000. Energy and performance aspects in sport surfaces. *Sporterletzung-Sportschaden* 14: 82–89.

Tabata, Izumi, Kouji Nishimura, Motoki Kouzaki, Yuusuke Hirai, Futoshi Ogita, Motohiko Miyachi, and Kaoru Yamamoto. 1996. Effects of moderate-intensity endurance and high-intensity intermittent training on anaerobic capacity and VO$_2$max. *Medicine & Science in Sports & Exercise* 28 (10): 1327–30.

Van Mechelen, Willem. 1994. Injuries in running. *Clinical Practice of Sports Injury Prevention and Care,* 421–44. London: Blackwell Scientific Publications.

Van Middelkoop, M., J. Kolkman, J. Van Ochten, S. M. A. Bierma-Zeinstra, and B. Koes. 2008. Prevalence and incidence of lower extremity injuries in male marathon runners. *Scandinavian Journal of Medicine & Science in Sports* 18 (2) (April): 140–44.

Wilk, B., S. Nau, and B. Valero. 2009. Physical therapy management of running injuries using an evidenced-based functional approach. *American Medical Athletic Association Journal* (January): 36–38.

Recommended Reading

Balk, Malcolm. *Master the Art of Running.* London: Collins & Brown, 2009.

Dreyer, Danny, and Katherine Dreyer. *ChiRunning: A Revolutionary Approach to Effortless, Injury-Free Running.* New York: Simon & Schuster, 2004.

Heggie, Jack. *Running with the Whole Body: A 30-Day Program to Running Faster with Less Effort.* Berkeley: North Atlantic Books, 1996.

Lydiard, Arthur, and Garth Gilmour. *Run the Lydiard Way.* London: Hodder & Stoughton, 1978.

Lydiard, Arthur, and Garth Gilmour. *Running with Lydiard.* 2nd ed. London: Meyer & Meyer Sport, 2000.

McDougall, Christopher. *Born to Run: A Hidden Tribe, Superathletes, and the Greatest Race the World Has Never Seen.* New York: Knopf, 2009.

Murphy, Sam, and Sarah Connors. *Running Well.* Champaign, IL: Human Kinetics, 2008.

Romanov, Nicholas, with John Robson. *Dr. Nicholas Romanov's Pose Method of Running.* Miami: Pose Tech Press, 2004.

Index

About the Authors

Danny Abshire is the cofounder of Newton Running and a passionate lifelong runner. A longtime running form coach and injury expert, he has worked closely with thousands of athletes from beginners to Olympians, helping them improve their form and technique. Danny started Active Imprints in 1988, making custom orthotics for elite and age-group runners and triathletes. He lives in Boulder, Colorado, with his wife and two sons.

Brian Metzler has run more than 50,000 miles in his life, tested more than 750 pairs of running shoes, and raced just about every distance from 50 yards to 100 miles. He is a senior editor at *Running Times* and has written about endurance sports for *Runner's World, Triathlete, Inside Triathlon, Men's Health, Men's Journal,* and *Outside;* was the founding editor and associate publisher of *Trail Runner* and *Adventure Sports* magazines; and is the author of *Running Colorado's Front Range.*

ALSO AVAILABLE FROM VELOPRESS

UNLOCK YOUR SPEED

THE WORKOUTS IN A BINDER® SERIES

RUN
WORKOUTS
For Runners and Triathletes

BOBBY MCGEE
with Marathon Plans by Mark Plaatjes

Spiral-bound sweatproof pages | 5" x 7" | 200 pp. | $29.95 | 978-1-934030-33-2

ALL TOO OFTEN, runners and triathletes fall into a running rut, stuck in the same gear and unable to break out. The key to unlocking your speed is running a variety of workouts.

This season you can reach new levels of speed and endurance using 80 fresh and challenging workouts in *Run Workouts for Runners and Triathletes*. Mixing it up with track repeats, hill runs, and interval workouts, world-class running and triathlon coach Bobby McGee and world champion marathoner Mark Plaatjes give runners of all stripes a complete collection of workouts and training plans.

Stop running in circles. Break out with *Run Workouts for Runners and Triathletes*.

Forewords by Tim Noakes and Samantha McGlone

Available in bookstores, tri and running shops, and online.
Learn more about VeloPress books for runners and download free samples at velopress.com/running.

ALSO AVAILABLE FROM VELOPRESS

PERSONAL RECORD

Paperback with 2-color interior | 6½" x 9" | 232 pp. | $15.95 | 978-1-934030-36-3

NEXT TO RUNNING shoes, a training diary is the most important piece of training equipment a runner owns. Whether training to set a PR in a 5K race or to complete your first marathon, runners of all abilities will gain insight into their fitness and performance with *The Runner's Diary* by running coach Matt Fitzgerald. This two-color training diary offers plenty of space for key data like resting heart rate, mileage, pace/splits, intensity, aches and pains, and workout ratings.

Before you lace up your running shoes again, start planning your next PR with *The Runner's Diary*.

Available in bookstores, tri and running shops, and online.
Learn more about VeloPress books for runners and download free samples at velopress.com/running.